WAKE UP

WAKE UP

How to Practice Zen Buddhism

Bonnie Myotai Treace

ROCKRIDGE
PRESS

Interior and Cover Designer: Will Mack
Art Producer: Sue Smith
Editor: Vanessa Ta
Production Editor: Edgar Doolan

Illustrations: © 2019 EkaterinaYa/Shutterstock (eye); Maxim Ibragimov/Shutterstock (all textures)

ISBN: Print 978-1-64152-390-5 | eBook 978-1-64152-391-2

For Peter Matthiessen, whom I first met when he'd forgotten his bessu (Zen priest socks with ankle snaps). He borrowed mine, which were way too small, and flapped about while he processed and bowed conducting a very formal ceremony in front of hundreds.

You were the deepest smile, unflappable even when flapping. May all our Zen be just so.

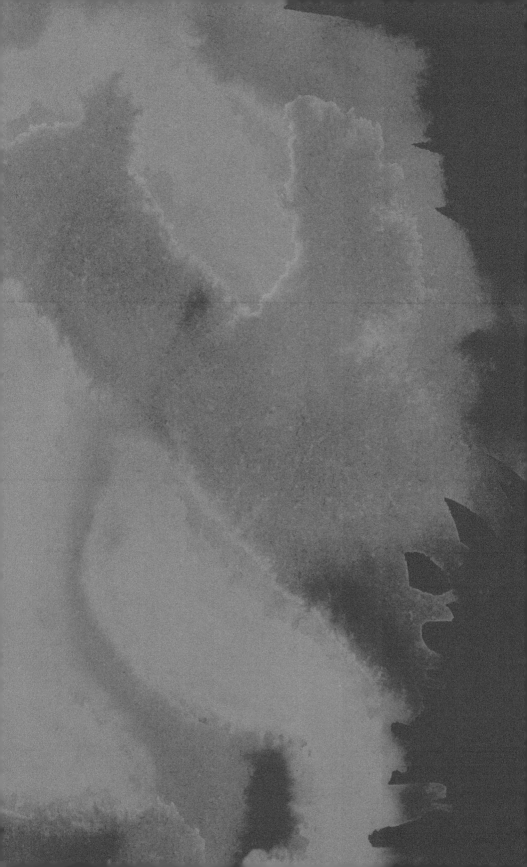

Contents

Introduction

TO STUDY ZEN IS TO STOP RUNNING. You sit down
with yourself, take a deep breath, take off the mask usually
used to hide your pain, and begin to get real. You begin to
devote yourself to waking up from what can only be called
the trance of habit. Zen practice is a confrontation with the
persistent dream that certainty is possible; it is an invitation to
relax into a vast unknowing. You begin to see how intoxicating
opinions and objects are and commit to a "spiritual sobriety"
informed by spaciousness and silence.

With Zen practice also comes a direct experience of your life
as not separate from all other life, which means a tremendous
yet tender strength becomes your own. As you stop running
from every discomfort—yours or others'—your relationship
to suffering is transformed. Compassion and kindness become
more natural than fear and anger.

In this book, we'll open up how Zen practice works. We'll
look a bit at its history, as well as the place it occupies in Buddhism, world religions, and culture more widely. We'll look into
its traditional "shapes and forms" but emphasize how to bring
it home, to keep it intimately real in this moment. We'll do
this because, essentially, Zen can only be understood by practicing it. Everything else is description. And though knowing

something about Zen may be interesting, until we put our own body and breath into it, it doesn't really begin to address our lives.

I found that true for myself. After years of a kind of noodling around with meditation on my own, I hit a point when I wanted to drench myself in its deepest waters, and I moved to a Zen monastery. Zen has a tradition of cutting through sentimentality, and monasticism implies a single, deep intention shaping a community—both spoke to me. And I liked that working with a teacher was central to Zen study; I wouldn't be allowed to drift or hide. It was 1983.

Twenty-plus years later, I had lived decades as a monastic, become a priest, and been designated a Zen teacher (Sensei). I completed formal study with my teacher, was named the first "dharma successor" in my order, and then continued study with several other teachers. I founded a lay Zen center in NYC and oversaw the purchase and renovation of a building (temple) there. After teaching in the city for about ten years, I started a nonresidential training program called Hermitage Heart with students throughout the United States.

All to say, I've had the great honor (and challenge!) of studying with many wonderful teachers and thousands of students in varied situations for almost 40 years. I've seen people change the way they live and die, face illness, and experience the incredible stressors of our time. I've watched as prisoners find the freedom implicit in their mind and patients with debilitating disease find uncommon peace. For all of us, though, it begins with a commitment to wake up. What does that look like?

Most people will find that their enchantment with ego is like a spell that gets broken each time they engage in genuine practice.

An alternative begins to wake up in the heart-mind—a glimpse of something truer, more honest. Breaking from the ego-trance, even momentarily, wakes up a bone-deep calmness: The tension of pretending can be let go, again and again.

If you find yourself drawn to explore Zen practice, you have likely become aware of, or even deeply despaired, the opposite of waking up: the quiet, pervasive sense of being disconnected, stuck in some shade of trance. It's all too easy to waste this unique, precious, and wild life searching in vain for something, anything, to make it better or easier. We run ourselves ragged trying to improve, trying to get to one goal after another, none of which really does the trick. We're always striving and restless, and nothing quite satisfies. No matter how we try to avoid it, the question *Who am I?* finds us on sleepless nights, or in moments of grief or awe.

Come to these pages as you might to a monastery: with your deepest existential questions alive in your heart, forming "the great matter at hand." Be ready to sit down in the center of your life, see clearly, and release the patterns of fear that hold you back. I offer my complete support and faith that you can. Awakening is your birthright.

This book is about how Zen practice can inform and inspire your everyday life—even as it is filled with jobs, family, friends, art, and humor, and takes place amid the civilizational crises of climate chaos, war, racism, misogyny, and the excesses and injustices of capitalism. Every moment delivers a question about who we really are. I have found that the deepest water is this very life and that it actually doesn't require a geographic shift—only and utterly that we dive in completely right where we are.

ONE

What Is Zen?

The word *Zen* is provocative in a number of ways. This is a good thing, especially for those who are hoping to not just gather another vocabulary word but to actually address existential suffering, both our own and that of others. One might think, given the way the word is bandied about in popular culture, advertising, and design, that Zen is simply about simplicity. Zen has even been bizarrely appropriated to sell everything from perfume to wine to cars. But an old teaching says, "Zen is not what you think it is. Of course, neither is it otherwise." Though mainstream culture seems to have satisfied itself that Zen means *chill out*, please be encouraged to delve in more thoroughly.

Zen began as a tradition that doesn't "rely on words and letters." From the get-go, Zen has had this bold insistence on getting through to the truth and not getting waylaid by mere descriptions or names for that truth. Many say Zen is about coming back to the moment, but the question remains con-stant: What really is the moment? How is the past—our history of failings and strivings—included in this raw moment? How is the future—our personal and civilizational consequences and obligations—included in how we wake up, moment by moment?

For centuries in varied countries and cultures, Zen has been embraced as a way of realizing who we really are, what this life is, and how to live it with vibrance, courage, and subtlety. Yet we're in a particular and critical time in human history: a time when even the continuation of sentient life on our planet beyond the next 100 years depends on how we understand who we are and how we serve life. How might Zen help us to clarify our own lives and priorities and support this new understanding? We'll start by dispelling some false notions, review a bit of Zen's history, traditional teachings, and basic methods, and then take up how Zen might come home to where we each sit.

What Is Zen Not?

One big key as we arrive at the threshold of Zen practice is to notice that we've likely brought along our bag of expectations. Each of us arrives with all sorts of ideas. Zen is this, not that; liturgy is relevant for the monks, not laypeople; a teacher should work this way, not that way; I should feel better, not worse . . . and hey, isn't this about being imperturbable? As genuine practice begins, the bag will get turned over, spilled out (many times!) so that we can see what we're carrying, what unessential ideas we are dragging along with us. It may hurt when this happens—the poetic descriptions of Zen don't always let us know that. Yet as the burden of expectation begins to release, there is a kind of lightening up. We find we can lean into the journey, without needing it to be exactly what we thought it would be. We get out of our heads and into our lived experience.

So, the caveat: Be careful not to go into Zen practice to gather up new things, new concepts, new ambitions. And when you notice that *is* what you're doing (because this is the way our minds naturally work), pause and set down your bag for a moment. Notice that the idea of "getting something" or "going somewhere" is likely beginning to weigh you down and is taking you away from where you are.

Let's look at some of the misconceptions you may run into. As Zen began being taught and practiced on American shores in the 1950s and '60s, its cut-no-corners, gentle-*cum*-fierce, and generally iconoclastic character appealed deeply to a culture undergoing revolutions of antiauthoritarianism. American converts flocked to Zen centers. Chinese, Tibetan, Korean, and Japanese teachers of Buddhism seemed to embody both gentle confidence and spiritual depth, which attracted students into committed study.

This is also how the limiting image of Zen wisdom being a male, Eastern elder in monk's robes formed in popular culture. The Asian teachers came from lineages refined in monastic community; in America, most convert students were lay householders, combining career and family with Zen practice. Almost all the Asian teachers were monks and came from countries where male privilege was normative.

For decades in the United States, heavily hierarchical administration of training centers, with one "authority" at the top making all decisions, went largely unquestioned. This happened partly because it was difficult for American students and teachers alike to distinguish skillful teachings from the teaching styles imported largely unintentionally with them. So, Zen in America has had some significant growing pains over its several decades as this Eastern tradition became rooted in Western soil.

As always, however, it returns to where each one of us stands—honestly facing whatever barriers lie in our path, ready to take up our freedom.

Master Wu-men, known for his koan collection *The Gateless Gate,* spoke to this:

> *Gateless is the ultimate Way;*
> *there are thousands of ways to it.*
> *If you pass through this barrier,*
> *You may walk freely in the universe.*

Also, take note that there is no issue with integrating Zen into what may already be your religious or spiritual practice. Thomas Merton, the Trappist monk known for exploring Zen along with his Catholicism, famously wrote that comparing Zen to Christianity is like comparing tennis to mathematics. They are different playing fields. One can play tennis and still be a mathematician. Christians can practice Zen, without leaving their Christianity. You don't need to get rid of your "tennis shoes" or your "quadratic equations"—just be a mathematician playing tennis, if you will. There are many Jewish Zen practitioners (hence, *JewBu* is a thing), as well as meditators from many other religious traditions.

WHAT IS KARMA?

Karma is not a synonym for consequences, though pop culture tends to use the word that way. Karma is actually the universal law of cause and effect. It links an action's underlying intention to that action's consequences; it equates the actions of body, speech, and thought as potential sources of karmic consequences.

In other words, as one of my teachers used to say, "What you do and what happens to you are the same thing." Intentions matter. What we do matters. If anyone is harmed, we are harmed. (And more positively, if anyone is relieved of their suffering, we are likewise.)

In other words, there is no separation. Life is intimate.

Awakening and morality cannot be separated.

Early on, as Zen first began taking root in the United States, misconceptions about karma ran rampant. Statements that "Zen is beyond morality," made by distinguished scholars, directed people away from the reality that, in this one great universe, we sink or swim together, not alone. No one person or thing is apart from this shared reality and responsibility.

The study of karma is intrinsic to genuine Zen study. In training, the study of the Buddhist Precepts (moral and ethical teachings) is taken very seriously, and the implications of karma are explored throughout one's lifetime.

What Is Zen?

All the teachings of Zen are called *upaya,* or *skillful means.* They are designed to help us see and realize that the truth we are seeking is already present. Because the truth is non-dual (not two, not either/or), we can say there is no one to give and no one to receive. This is why you'll sometimes hear it said that "there are no Zen teachers"—only the truth itself. Because of this radical oneness, there is never a time that truth does not exist that is separate from a time when it does. There is never a time realization exists separate from when it does not. This moment touches and interpenetrates with all moments. This is why a Zen teaching may ask: "Past, present, and future meet in a body: What is that body?" It is also clear that there's a huge difference between believing in the non-dual (and its implications) and fully, inarguably experiencing it. So, *upaya* evolved to evoke the realization of truth, rather than to explain it.

Zen has been called a peculiar religious tradition. There is even long-standing debate about calling it a religion at all. It doesn't require worship, belief in doctrines, or devotion. It isn't theistic, but it's not atheistic or agnostic either: It simply doesn't take up the subject of God. The Buddha is understood as an ordinary human being who freed himself from the burden of quintessential suffering and then taught others about the possibility of doing likewise.

In one sense, Zen traces itself back to Siddhartha Gautama, who was born over 2,500 years ago into a royal family in Nepal. He led a very sheltered life and then one day traveled outside the palace gates—and all his assumptions were fundamentally disrupted by the realities of old age, sickness, and death. No longer sure of what life was actually about, he left his home, gave away all his belongings, shaved his head, and put on simple robes. He lived in utmost simplicity and studied with the great teachers of the day. He was not so different from, though perhaps more thoroughgoing than, those of us today who start our spiritual search in earnest and then hit the road seeking answers, teachers, and methods.

But nothing that Siddhartha learned fully addressed the deepest questions he had. Eventually, he decided to sit as he had long before as a child: under a tree, without reaching for anything, without restricting himself in any way.

He would stay there until he felt genuine peace. And, the story goes, one night, after many days and nights, as he saw the morning star, he realized *anuttara-samyak-sambodhi*—great and perfect enlightenment—and would then be known as Buddha Shakyamuni (Greatly awakened being of the Shakya clan).

Initially, all Shakyamuni said was how incredible it was that "all beings have awakened nature . . . in one moment, I and all beings together have entered the Way (of enlightenment)." He had no inclination to create a new religion. But his fellow long-suffering monks saw his transformation and begged him to teach. Being asked by heartfelt companions, he was called to begin the impossible task of "teaching what cannot be taught."

Another juncture when Zen can be said to "begin" is about 300 years after the *buddhadharma* (Buddha's true teaching) crossed from India to China and was invigorated by the great sage Bodhidharma. It was around the year 520 CE when Bodhidharma introduced the specific teachings that are regarded as the taproot of the Zen school. Much of Bodhidharma's biography is likely the stuff of legend, yet there are numerous early records of a wise monk who brought the Buddhist tradition back to its authentic vitality.

WHAT IS ZAZEN?

Zazen (literally *sitting meditation*) is a form of silent meditation that can be understood in several ways. In one sense, it is a method to achieve enlightenment. You become still, you concentrate body, breath, and mind, and you set a clear intention. In another sense, though, zazen is a direct and clear expression of the practitioner's already-awakened, undivided nature. So, to do zazen is both to seek the truth and to embody it. In both of these senses, zazen is the real heart of Zen practice.

The great Zen master Dogen said, "To study the Buddha Way is to study the self, to study the self is to forget the self, and to forget the self is to be awakened by the ten thousand things." Essentially, zazen is the study of the self. To be enlightened by the ten thousand things—the myriad joys and sorrows of this embodied human life—is to recognize that oneself and all things are one.

The historic Buddha awakened in seated meditation. This archetype of sitting down—resting, if you will—in the truth that is ever-present is Zen's central image. Zen spread from India to China, to Japan, to other parts of Asia, and then finally to the West. It is a simple practice, yet in its simplicity there is untold depth.

The most famous of Bodhidharma's teachings, and what many consider the essence of Zen, can be found in these four points:

Zen is a special transmission outside the scriptures,
Not depending on words and letters;
Directly pointing to the mind,
Seeing its nature and becoming Buddha

Of course, Zen also can be said to begin every time anyone wholeheartedly practices. The word *Zen* (non-dual meditation) makes clear that meditative practice is central, even as it challenges the notions we may have about what meditation comprises.

But let's start by looking into the very first formal teaching of the Buddha, the first "turning of the dharma wheel," called the Four Noble Truths and the Eightfold Path.

The Four Noble Truths

Of all the possible ways the Buddha could have begun his teaching, the way he did so is somewhat counterintuitive. He gave his first discourse at the Deer Park in Sarnath. He could have started with words about freedom, love, and wonder. Instead, the Buddha's first teaching acknowledged that life is essentially suffering. And not just "sometimes in some ways"—no, his point was that humans are always, due to the impermanent nature of all things and the grasping it inspires, somewhat or profoundly ill at ease.

The Sanskrit word *dukkha,* which we translate as "suffering," has a broader meaning as well. It points to the pervasive sense of dissatisfaction about things not being as one wants. It includes the shadow of discomfort existing even in times when we do have what we want, but know that change is unstoppable and there is no way to secure our pleasant situation. This "dis-ease" was the first of his Four Noble Truths.

Was the Buddha trying to depress the monks by emphasizing suffering and dissatisfaction in his first offering? It certainly doesn't seem to be a good sales pitch to start a new religious venture. Many, upon first hearing of this first truth, assume Buddhism will be hopelessly pessimistic. But the Buddha, like a good doctor, was simply starting with a diagnosis based on the actual, if not often acknowledged, human condition that each and every one of us shares; then, having gotten the patient's attention, he offers medicine. In other words, if we try to skip over the reality of our own pain, our practice will be forever weak: We can't encounter truth until we get true with ourselves. He said, "Both in the past, and now, I have set forth only this: dukkha and the end of dukkha."

So, it is important to note that the Buddha didn't end his discourse on a hopeless note, but rather continued with the very good news of the Four Noble Truths: 1) life suffers dis-ease, 2) this dis-ease has a cause, 3) it is possible to relieve this dis-ease, and 4) the path to that relief. Let's see what these four teachings really point to and how they might inform our daily practice.

FIRST NOBLE TRUTH: LIFE SUFFERS
When the young prince Siddhartha went on his first jour-ney out of the protected palace in which he had lived all his youth, he encountered four sights that brought about a shift from innocence toward a more mature awareness. His story of encountering these sights models the process of how our lives

WHAT IS SUFFERING?

Buddha talked about three kinds of suffering. The first is linked to the first three sights the Buddha saw on his first journey outside his palace: old age, sickness, and death—the suffering of painful experiences. A second was suffering caused by the fact of constant change—we inevitably lose the things, people, and situations to which we become attached and experience the stress of not being able to secure ourselves to anything permanent. Even in states of pleasure, we know things will change. The third was the suffering of existential unease—when we sense we're not really awake to our true nature.

Buddha taught that everyone is subject to suffering. What happens when we accept that everyone inevitably hurts in these ways? Perhaps our own suffering becomes less of a personal affront. Perhaps we taste a bit of kind commiseration or empathy. At the very least, we're freed from a kind of pretense and denial.

The Buddha said: Start by taking suffering in. Notice it in the most complete way possible. In our culture, with its tendency to cast blame on those suffering poverty, chronic illness, overwork, aging, etc., it may be especially challenging to slow down and really register this first truth of the Buddha's teaching. Given that, it is especially important, if we seek the truth, to take that challenge.

come to include the poignant realities of vulnerability, lack, aging, and death. What did he see?

First, an old man, suffering the fragility and decline of body and mind that aging brings. Then, a very ill person, suffering the pains of disease to which we are all vulnerable. And finally, a dead person, who suffered the loss of life itself. As he struggled to integrate all this suffering into what had to that point been a naive and privileged worldview, he also saw a holy person, someone who had devoted their life to ultimate truth.

For the young prince, these four sights meant one thing: He could no longer live having not seen them. His innocence, and any denial of the suffering all sentient life is subject to, was over. He'd been shaken forcibly from one kind of trance: that he or anyone could be safe, immune to life's shadow. He had left "the palace"—the place in his heart that was walled off from vulnerability and impermanence—and began his spiritual journey in earnest.

SECOND NOBLE TRUTH: SUFFERING HAS A CAUSE

From its beginnings, the key insight of Buddhism has been that the way we normally live, in terms of a separate "self," causes great suffering. When we identify as a separate self, immediately everything the self needs is by definition "out there," and we've got a recipe for nonstop craving and isolation. This is the Second Noble Truth: The cause of suffering arises from this habit of separating what is actually and always whole.

Still, the Second Noble Truth is easily misunderstood. It is usually translated as "the cause of suffering is craving and attachment." But when we're suffering a toothache, how does it help to be told that the cause is "my personal craving" not to have excruciating pain and my "selfish attachment" to feeling good? We wouldn't want dental care based on such blithe advice . . . nor a spiritual path. So we need to see deeply into what's at play here. We need to be caring and careful, in order to not add more suffering to what is already present (and hurts, like a sore tooth or worse!). Discernment is subtle, but be clear: It never demands being cruel to oneself, but rather being in a radical integrity where this body and all bodies are cared for.

When the Buddha taught that there is a cause to suffering and that it comes from our holding on to a particular, solid sense of the self, he wasn't being glib. He wasn't denying that an infant goes through the natural developmental stage of becoming an individual within surroundings, with a functioning dynamic of "inner world" and "outer world," an internal space confronted by a space beyond the borders of the skin. He was, however, pointing to the possibility of seeing more completely and not confusing our sense of selfhood with ultimate reality. He taught that we could also realize a kind of equilibrium in which the body exists, impacted by but not apart from the environment. The key to that equilibrium? Not attaching wholly to our self-view.

THIRD NOBLE TRUTH: SUFFERING CAN END

The Buddha did not just teach the truth of suffering—he, quite radically, taught the relief of suffering. He was addressing the profound mental suffering we feel when the habit of holding on (often as if our life depended on it) comes up against the flowing stream of life. Our habit is to again and again seek out a kind of idol, a thing that will solve our sensed lack of connectedness and permanence . . . and we can do that with absolutely anything—a relationship, a better job, health, Christ, even the idea of enlightenment. It's only when we leave the market where "this-is-the-thing-I-need-to-be-whole" is bought and sold that our suffering eases. The seeking, the shopping, and the idol-making put what we need forever on the outside.

The Buddha taught that in any experience, we can, in a sense, come home to the reality that nothing is outside (nor inside, for that matter). There is no ultimate line. Face-to-face with suffering, how does that really work? How does it work in the midst of tremendous pain and disappointment? Isn't it natural to run away into distractions and addictions? But if there is nowhere to run, the possibility is that this moment and place is It. Is home. Every moment: thus. This is why the Buddha taught not to deny the moments of pain, but instead, in the barest of ways, to acknowledge them, to put no distance between oneself and them, or any state. He's not saying that we should become resigned to suffering and fall into apathy, but rather that we open our hearts to include everything, without that habitual distance and without judgment.

The Third Noble Truth is that by not separating our self from things—even noble things, even painful things—we embody our wholeness. But how does one "not separate" oneself, especially from painful things? In his Fourth Noble Truth, the Buddha talks about the ways to do just that.

FOURTH NOBLE TRUTH: THE PATH TO END SUFFERING
The fourth of the Noble Truths basically follows up on the first three: There is suffering, it has a cause, it's possible to relieve it, and now, here is the way or "path" to doing so. The Buddha presented a path that has eight different parts (the Eightfold Path) in order to make clear that absolutely every aspect of our life, activity, understanding, and attitude would be involved in waking up.

WHAT IS SAMSARA?

Buddhism teaches that *samsara* arises from living in terms of a false notion: the idea that our ego is a single, separate entity with an unchanging essence. Because we believe in, and function in terms of, this ego, we can waste a lifetime defending it. We generate anger and fear when we perceive a threat to it, we use others to satisfy its hungers, and we live with a basic indifference to those not useful to it. In other words, we are busy causing ourselves and others endless suffering. This rather sad, seemingly endless process is called samsara. We create an ego-defined world, place ourselves in it, and eventually it falls apart, over and over and over again. Samsara has a taste of being trapped in a story we can't get out of.

Samsara is also a bit of a coyote. Most of us would scoff at the idea that we might find some thing or person that will "solve" all our problems, yet what our words deny, our days reveal as our project. Put up a barrier or proscription to having some "needed thing," and we need it all the more. Prohibit a drug (or a relationship) and voilà: That's what we crave; having it would make things perfect. Tell a child he can't have a toy: That toy becomes the only thing he wants, and he wants it in every cell in his body. Put the capacities of perfect health beyond reach, or desired weight, or . . . and samsara spins and twists our lives into sadness.

When the Buddha taught the Eightfold Path in his first sermon after his enlightenment, he faced an excruciating assignment. He saw the discontent of the monks gathered around asking that he give instruction and inspiration; he could not turn away. Their pain was evident. They were caught in samsara ("wandering" through the veils of illusion).

But how do you give what can't be given? Though the Eightfold Path is sometimes treated as a sort of "how-to" map to reach enlightenment, it's important to recognize that, though it is a sobering message in many ways, it also arrives with a kind of wink. The path must be taken, and it doesn't lead somewhere else. The metaphor of a path is a paradox—it takes you on a journey to the center of being, which you've never been apart from and couldn't leave if you tried. For this reason, it is sometimes called a "pathless path" or a "path without a goal." The path is leading you squarely back to yourself, albeit with a new awareness of what that self is.

The Eightfold Path

The Eightfold Path looks like a list of eight discrete steps, but the order is random and each aspect of the path complements and amplifies every other aspect. Like flower petals enfolded to create a blossom, each "fold," or petal, has a unique position and all of them together create something greater than the parts individually.

Each aspect of the path is an area of practice meant to be brought to realization. (In fact, one of my teachers created a training program called the *Eight Gates*, considered a modern expression of the Eightfold Path.)

Right in this teaching is not *right* as opposed to *wrong*. The word translated as *right*, *samyanc* (Sanskrit) or *samma* (Pāli), means *wise*, *wholesome*, *skillful*, and *ideal*. It describes something that is complete and coherent. It's helpful, too, to understand *right* in the same sense we might talk about how a boat riding the waves can "right itself."

The Path is divided into three main sections: wisdom, ethical conduct (discipline/disposition), and mental discipline.

THE EIGHTFOLD PATH

THE WISDOM PATH

Right View

Right Intention

THE ETHICAL CONDUCT PATH

Right Speech

Right Action

Right Livelihood

THE MENTAL DISCIPLINE PATH

Right Effort

Right Mindfulness

Right Concentration

The Wisdom Path: Right View and Right Intention comprise the wisdom path. Right View is about perceiving the true nature of ourselves and the world around us. Right Intention is about commitment that penetrates down to our bones, speech, thoughts, and silence.

The Ethical Conduct Path: Right Speech, Right Action, and Right Livelihood call us to take care in our speech, our actions, and our daily lives to not only do no harm to others and cultivate wholesomeness in ourselves, but also to stand for and speak on behalf of others as called. This part of the path relates to the Precepts (or principles), which describe the way an enlightened being conducts their life in the world.

The Mental Discipline Path: Mental discipline and seeing through delusion is realized through Right Effort, Right Mindfulness, and Right Concentration. Meditation, in both its seated and active forms, is identified with this part of the path.

RIGHT VIEW

One of the first books I've always recommended to new students is *What the Buddha Taught* by Theravada scholar Walpola Rahula. In it he calls this first of the Eightfold Path practices "seeing a thing in its true nature, without name and label." So, Right View is the naked truth, if you will. Right View shows us life outside the trance and makes possible, because it is not content with artifice, both genuine love and genuine peace.

In a way, both our happiness and the happiness of those around us actually depend upon the degree to which we bring Right View to life. It begins when we shift away from being okay with the suffering we create by basing everything on our mixed-up perceptions. It is practiced when we commit to the ongoing clearing out of our confusion, misunderstanding, and deluded thinking.

RIGHT INTENTION

The Buddha taught that what we think—along with what we say and how we act—creates karma, which creates our life. In this way, intention is critically important. Right Intention together with Right Understanding make up the *Wisdom Aspect*, the parts of the Eightfold Path that cultivate *prajna* (direct insight, non-discriminating knowledge).

THREE KINDS OF RIGHT INTENTION

1. Renunciation—which counters attachment. The Diamond Sutra famously says, "Thus shall you regard this fleeting world: a drop of dew, a bubble floating in a stream; a flash of lightning in a summer cloud, a flickering lamp, an illusion, a phantom, or a dream."

   All people need housing, clothing, food, and medical care (and too many do not have them). Some people have access to much more than the essentials. We get lost, however, when we forget that all of it is that flash of lightning, a drop of momentary dew. To find that dew, radiant and luminous, presented on the grass tips of this life is good fortune; to try to hold onto that dew as the sun rises is confused and impossible. Letting it be and letting it go is the renunciation of Right Intention.

2. Goodwill (loving-kindness or *metta*)—which counters ill will. To cultivate a love that does not discriminate between good and worthless beings, a love in which rejection and alienation fall away, akin to the unconditional love (idealized) parents feel for their child: This is the goodwill of Right Intention.

3. Harmlessness—which counters harmfulness. The Sanskrit word for *non-harming* is *ahimsa,* and it describes a practice of not doing violence to anything. Not creating harm also requires *karuna,* or compassion, which is an active sympathy, a willingness to bear and respond to the pain of others as oneself. When the bug you squash (or the person you hurt) is recognized as yourself, the harmlessness of Right Intention enters practice.

RIGHT SPEECH

The practice of Right Speech is wholehearted expression. It is being silent when that is the right thing to do, and it is also speaking without holding back on behalf of others when called on to do so. It also means not failing to express the beauty and poetry of life. It is not, as some seem to propose, a practice of being consistently soft-spoken and never saying anything controversial. It includes being both fierce and yielding, as conditions warrant.

We're in particularly demanding times. Our media, both social and civic, is now largely designed to deceive and confuse, and communication in general is increasingly unkind. The points of view of women and of other disenfranchised people are too often absent or distorted. We can create violent language, thoughts, and actions, which will mingle together and amplify each other. Or we can practice peace-generating, clarifying, and inclusive words, thoughts, and actions, which will support one another and life itself. The latter is the practice of Right Speech.

As recorded in the Pāli Canon, the historical Buddha taught that Right Speech had four parts:

1. Abstaining from false speech—not telling lies, deceiving, or leaving out essential details.

2. Not slandering others or using words in ways that cause enmity.

3. Not using rude or abusive language.

4. Not indulging in idle talk or gossip.

These cautions also have another side: using language truthfully and honestly; using language with goodwill, in the direction of the greatest truth.

We also cannot really practice Right Speech if we don't practice *right listening*; the two are interdependent. Our speech is not ours alone: It happens between and among all of us. How deeply we hear, as well as how we choose to speak, reflects and creates reality. What reality will we choose to create?

RIGHT ACTION

Right Action is one of the three ethical conduct aspects of the Eightfold Path. The word for *action* is *karma* and means *volitional action*—things we choose to do. When we act "rightly," we act without selfish attachment to our own agendas. Right Action means being accurate or skillful, and it carries a connotation of *coherence* or *wisdom*.

Right Action often is supported by making vows to take up the Buddhist Precepts. Different schools of Buddhism have different lists of Precepts (often in Zen training *The Sixteen Bodhisattva Precepts* are studied, for instance), but in common to all the schools are these five:

1. Not killing

2. Not stealing

3. Not misusing sex

4. Not lying

5. Not abusing intoxicants

Most teachers, myself included, have expanded the ancient Precepts to have a positive edge, not just what looks like a list of don'ts. These are Vietnamese Zen teacher Thich Nhat Hanh's Five Mindfulness Trainings, which correlate to the five Precepts listed above:

1. Respect life. In awareness of the suffering caused by the destruction of life, work to protect all living things.

2. Be generous. Give freely of one's time and resources where they are needed, without hoarding anything. Promote social justice and well-being for everyone.

3. Respect sexuality and honor the body. Also, be aware of the pain caused by sexual misconduct, honor commitments, and act to protect others from sexual exploitation.

4. Practice loving speech and deep listening. Through deep listening and Right Speech, tear down the barriers that separate.

5. Consume mindfully. Nourish oneself and others with healthful food, media, art, and entertainment, while avoiding addiction, overconsumption, and agitation.

Please be encouraged to take up these Precepts, letting them support you, and to study them with a Zen teacher and community, if possible, to help refine your practice. Consider taping them on your mirror as a daily reminder of waking up and the commitment to be in the world with a deepening sense of harmony and responsibility, letting your life express compassion for all beings.

RIGHT LIVELIHOOD

Right Livelihood is a way of making a living that doesn't harm others: It is, in one sense, impossible, and yet it is also of the gravest importance. Speaking to people of his time, the Buddha cautioned against five types of vocation—selling weapons, trafficking in human beings, selling meat, producing or selling intoxicants, and distributing poison. Taken in its wider interpretation, this list can help us today to reflect on whether our work would be considered Right Livelihood and, if not, to move our practice in that direction. Are we putting poison (thoughts, words, things) into the world, feeding people's various intoxications and excesses, participating in disrespect for living beings? What might beginning, or taking a step toward, our real work look like?

Thich Nhat Hanh again, with a reminder: "Our vocation can nourish our understanding and compassion or erode them.

Being conscious of the consequences, far and near, of the way we earn our living is Right Livelihood."

Again, the teaching also has a positive side; it's not just about avoiding doing harmful things. It is the imperative to find a way to make a living that truly supports life. How can we engage our work with our deepest intentions, with the understanding that all beings are interconnected, so that we honor, respect, and protect one another and the life of our planet?

RIGHT EFFORT

The traditional definition of Right Effort sounds old-fashioned: It is to exert oneself to "develop wholesome qualities and to release unwholesome qualities." Sometimes translated as Right Diligence (in Pāli, *samma vayamo*), its spirit is that we apply ourselves wholeheartedly, but also without falling into a hyper-vigilance that is hurtful. It is not about being hard on oneself, but points instead to the importance of reenergizing our practice again and again with fresh, calm commitment.

The Buddha taught four considerations as part of Right Effort. Essentially, they are a reminder to get started, work with whatever gets in the way, attend to the things that help, strengthen those things, and keep going:

1. Make the effort to *prevent* unwholesome qualities—especially greed, anger, and ignorance—from arising.

2. Exert effort to *extinguish* any unwholesome qualities that already have arisen.

3. Make the effort to *cultivate* skillful, or wholesome, qualities—especially generosity, loving-kindness,

and wisdom, the opposites of greed, anger, and ignorance—that have not yet arisen.

4. Exert effort to *strengthen* the wholesome qualities that have already arisen.

Seeing that this "effort around effort" could be misunderstood and do harm, the Buddha gave an example to his students. He said the effort one brings to practice should be akin to tuning a string instrument. If we let the strings get too loose, there won't be any music—we just plunk and plod along. But if we keep it all too tight, the strings will break . . . as will we. Finding that balance—not too tight, not too loose—is Right Effort.

RIGHT MINDFULNESS

Given that mindfulness has become such a confusing buzzword lately, let's clarify a bit what it is not. It is not simply attention—we are always paying attention to something, but we are not, therefore, necessarily mindful. It is not just consciousness itself—if you're alive, experiencing, and not under anesthesia, you are conscious but not necessarily mindful. Nor is it just intentional attention—we can direct attention without being especially mindful. Mindfulness is also not simply "the present moment." All mental events—whether memory of the past or imagination of the future, whether spiteful or forgiving—take place in the present. So what, then, is mindfulness?

Andrew Olendzki, scholar and teacher, has said it well:

> *Mindfulness is an inherently wholesome or healthy mental factor, so it cannot function at any moment when the*

WHAT IS MINDFULNESS?

Mindfulness involves focusing on the breath and noticing thoughts as they come and go. In the process, we learn not to identify with each passing thought. When we direct attention to our experience in the present moment with kindness and without judgment, the mind settles.

With a plethora of studios popping up all over the place to cash in on the "mindfulness" craze, many issues have arisen around what capitalism is bringing to this ancient Buddhist practice. Companies are attracted to reducing their health care costs by destressing their workers via mindfulness training, but there's often no commensurate attention paid to the unkind working environment generating workers' stress. Corporations have enhanced productivity as workers learn how to focus better with mindfulness, but is making more widgets faster actually what the world needs? Well-intentioned schools are introducing mindfulness to help adolescents with anger management, but they may not be paying equal attention to addressing the systemic injustices that cause that anger and frustration.

A recent CDC report affirms that the number of Americans who've tried mindfulness meditation has tripled since 2012. The practice is being offered in many schools, prisons, corporations, and health care facilities to improve well-being. Do people become kinder, more compassionate, just by practicing mindfulness? Not necessarily. The Zen stance is that we usually also benefit from a social vision, a big view that creates a call to compassionate activity.

*mind is under the influence of greed or hatred, even in
their mildest versions of favoring and opposing. Anytime
you want or don't want things to be a certain way, the
mind is not being mindful.*

—Andrew Olendzki, *Lion's Roar* online magazine (June 2017)

So, to clarify: Right Mindfulness is based in the intimacy
of all things, the non-dual, and thus expresses selflessness. As
a practice, Right Mindfulness means we take up "the whole
catastrophe"—the body, senses, thoughts, and surroundings—
as ripe places for realization. Leaving nothing out, being
inclusive to the utmost, rejecting no one and no thing: This is
Right Mindfulness.

RIGHT CONCENTRATION

The Pāli word translated into English as *concentration* is *samadhi*.
Daido Loori explains it like this:

*Samadhi is a state of consciousness that lies beyond wak-
ing, dreaming, or deep sleep. It is a slowing down of mental activity through single-pointed concentration and the
realization of complete intimacy moment by moment.*

—John Daido Loori, *Eight Gates of Zen*

It is often said that samadhi is "oneness with the object of
meditation"—in other words, there is no distinction between
the act of meditating and the object of meditation. But in Buddhism, Right Concentration is also sometimes called *objectless
samadhi*. This deep meditative state has a rich detailing in the
history of teaching, with levels and aspects that complement
(and can seem to contradict!) one another. Samadhi, as one of

the Eightfold Path practices, indicates a meditative practice of extraordinary depth.

The word samadhi derives from the root words *sam-a-dha,* meaning *to bring together.* One important point to appreciate is that, in the Buddhist path teachings, all concentrative states are not necessarily samadhi. We can concentrate on anything, including many horrible and harmful things. Right Concentration is, along with Right Effort and Right Mindfulness, associated not only with the kind of discipline we can bring to the mind, but it also implies that natural compassion is at play.

We've briefly explored a few key ideas and concepts associated with the worldview of Buddhism and the practice of Zen. What does any of this indicate, though, for those interested in practicing in their everyday life today? How does one actually enter practice?

In my book of dharma teachings, *Winter Moon,* I also wrote about what "entering practice" involves:

> In Zen, to be a student is to explore the threshold, the place where old and new meet in this very body . . . It is to explore the "liminal"—the realm in which we're touched beyond personality, beyond the limits of what we understand or may have assigned ourselves as our life. A practitioner of Zen is most basically one whose life is awakening each moment to that threshold, the still point where all the possibilities exist. To practice is to release oneself from the momentum of the past, the karma of what seems to be indicated as the only next step. It is to turn one's face toward the unknown as a way of life.

WHAT IS NIRVANA?

Nirvana is often translated as "blown out" or "extinguished." It refers to the state of having blown out the fiery energies that cause our suffering and dis-ease (*dukkha*). We all get burned by what are called "the triple fires" that create *dukkha*. In Buddhism, the fires are identified as greed, anger (or hatred), and ignorance of what's real.

As the Third Noble Truth reminds us, the fires are conditioned states, having a cause—so they can also be brought to an end. (Whatever has the quality of *starting* also has the quality or condition of *ending*, by definition.) What remains after the fires are blown out is *nirvana*. The Buddha taught that our most natural state is nirvana; it is the reality we return to when we stop feeding the craziness of our ideas and habits.

Let's look at what happens as the fires begin to calm down. The Buddhist understanding is that by realizing and practicing the teachings (the *dharma*), specifically the Eightfold Path, we essentially cool down and stop living as much in reactive, deluded patterns. Still, the embers remain warm, though perhaps not as hot as the flames we had previously allowed to keep us hopping around. Even those who are enlightened are cautioned to remember the residual heat "in the embers" and to keep practicing.

Nirvana, then, is a state that has never been absent—but is only brought to life through practice that happens moment by moment.

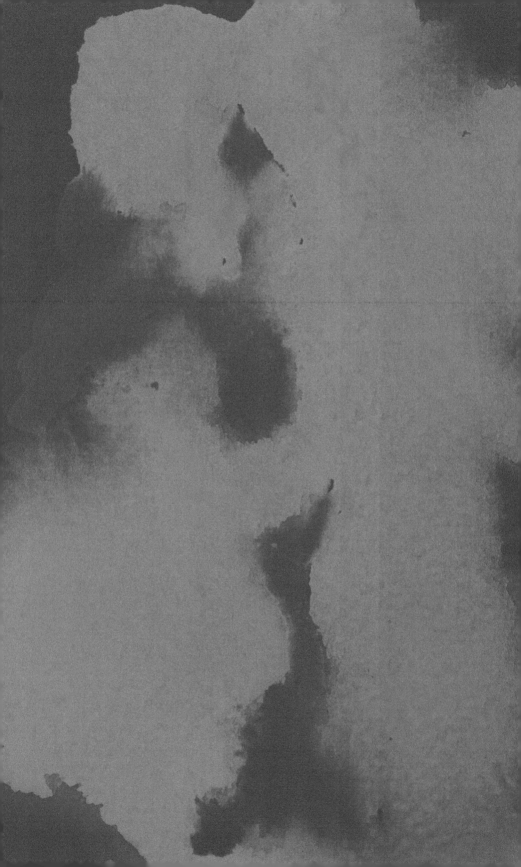

TWO

Zen Mind, Awakening Heart

It is helpful not to confuse what we know *about* Zen with Zen practice itself. In Zen, we call this Beginner's Mind (*bodhicitta*), Awakening Heart, or student mind. It's the basic position of spaciousness, an open-mindedness that is essentially curious and humble, willing to keep engaging the process of waking up. Waking up to—or as—what? Here we can say any number of things, none of which is "It"—our true nature, life as it is, wisdom, and compassion. The key is that whatever "answer" forms, we keep that process of awakening going. That is all, and of course, that is everything.

> *Now it is raining, but we don't know what will happen in the next moment. By the time we go out, it may be a beautiful day or a stormy day. Since we don't know, let's appreciate the sound of the rain now.*
>
> —Shunryu Suzuki, *Zen Mind, Beginner's Mind: Informal Talks on Zen Meditation and Practice*

I love this bit of wisdom from Shunryu Suzuki. It comes back to me often when I hear the rain (or find myself in or anticipating a storm of whatever kind). Suzuki is better known for another saying from the same collection of his talks: "In the beginner's mind there are many possibilities. In the expert's mind there are few." They both point to the same place—our capacity to come fresh to the moment and to not make a buffer between ourselves and the world. Also, they're a reminder to not let even our confidence and intelligence limit our possibilities.

Awakening Heart (*bodhicitta*) functions when we encounter pain in our life and remember that others also hurt just as we do. Also, it functions when things are pleasant, and instead of just focusing on ourselves, we consider others. It is particularly available to us when we are touched by gratitude or love. In any moment of tenderness, *bodhicitta* is always here. It is available each moment as we care for the small things—the dirty dish, the cell phone that connects us to the whole world, the snowfall, the muddy boot. When we drop the habit of resenting and complaining, it is very present. As we practice acknowledging these experiences, no matter how feeble this Awakening Heart may seem, it will, over time, grow stronger.

Beginner's Mind

Awakening Heart and Beginner's Mind can be used interchangeably—heart and mind are seen as one in Zen. They both refer to *bodhicitta*. What if instead of shutting down, thinking we know what's present or coming, the mind-heart remained ready, genuinely open for anything? Once Beginner's Mind becomes a reflexive practice, we'll more easily notice when the thought *I've got it now; I have attained something* starts blocking the view, sucking the air out of the room. Conversely, we'll notice when thoughts of *I'll never get this; I'm a failure* likewise block the view. (One of my teachers used to call me out when I'd express a lack of confidence, saying, "You know, putting yourself down is just as self-involved as thinking you're great.") To practice, we let these thoughts—and their thousands of variations—float down the stream of consciousness . . . just noticing them, without building a house on top of each one, moving in, and making an identity of them. So, the next moment arrives. It's the one where your practice lives. You notice.

Does this mean always pretending that you've never met the person you're with or that you've never sung this song before? Of course not. But it does mean becoming aware of how self-centered thoughts and precluding attitudes limit us. When we try to alleviate the altogether human background noise of vulnerability and lack by turning up the volume on our self-ideas, we're employing a failing strategy. It's not unlike how we keep our earphones in, music blasting, head down staring at the phone, looking for likes . . . while missing our only-happens-once life. "If you miss the moment, you miss your life," John Daido Loori used to say. Beginner's Mind is that: not missing the moment and not missing our lives.

A note while we're here: Zen is also not anti-intellectual. Though it emphasizes that enlightenment comes not through conceptualization but rather through direct insight, direct insight is also to be supported by study and understanding. The Zen tradition actually produced a rich body of literature which has become a part of its practice and teaching. Influential sutras are: the Platform Sutra, Vimalakirti Sutra, Avatamsaka Sutra, the Shurangama Sutra, and the Mahaparinirvana Sutra. There are also Chán transmission records, such as *The Records of the Transmission of the Lamp*; the recorded sayings of masters and encounter dialogues; and the koan collections, such as *The Gateless Gate* and *The Blue Cliff Record*. See page 51 and the Resources section (page 122) for further examples.

The Practice

In the pages ahead, we'll look at what a life of practicing Zen entails. We'll explore meditation more fully, examine the workings of a teacher-student relationship, sitting alone and in groups, rituals and practices, and how it all lands at the kitchen sink, the daily-ness of our lives, the ground under our feet.

The first step of practice is to take our life seriously. Shunryu Suzuki once said, in his chewy way, "Life is like stepping onto a boat which is about to sail out to sea and sink." We are mortal and very much don't want to waste our lives. Something shifts when acknowledging that becomes visceral.

I'm reminded of a format used at my old monastery to see if someone was ready to enter the training there. We called it "meeting with the guardian council," and basically it involved a prospective student sitting in front of a group of older students and being asked why they wanted to do this. Sometimes it would be clear that the person applying was just in the wrong place. Usually, when it was off, it was obvious—they'd be better met doing something else. But sometimes, the most interesting times, everyone in the room could feel that the person was utterly sincere but wasn't able yet to drop the mask and speak genuinely. They'd cite secondary things but never quite reach the heart of it. We were aware that, for some folks, the situation itself triggered anxious reactions, so we gave time to create a trusting atmosphere. At its best, the guardian council functioned as an archetype, a calling out into the vast sky. We'd

FROZEN ALIVE

Michael came to talk with me after having been through a yearlong battle with a disease that was "supposed" to take his life. He'd faced low odds of surviving even six months. He'd worked hard to feel sure that, if he did die, his legacy would continue after his death, that he could face death at peace, and that his relationships were loving. But now he was in different territory: He was highly likely to live. He said that while he had been occupied with dying, he had, in a certain sense, lost track of being alive. Though he was tremendously grateful, he said he felt he was never quite just at the breakfast table, just walking across the street, just working. Everything was laden, and he sensed something in him was frozen after the overwhelming year he'd been through.

As we explored the nature of practice, its sole requirement to be "in the moment that's here, not the one you want to trade it for," he began to settle again into Beginner's Mind. Nothing is special in Beginner's Mind; everything is just practice. Splendid moments, when we're at ease, we acknowledge and they pass. Crazy moments, when we're creeps and petty tyrants: acknowledged, allowed to go. Fears that roil and bite: acknowledge, release, return to the breath. It is never about being better. It is, however, about being real, and that means we bump into our freedom and, with it, our responsibility.

CONTINUED

Philosopher Jean-Paul Sartre famously wrote, "We are condemned to freedom." This means that we are not only responsible for what we do, but also for what we don't do, the things we postpone or fail to act on altogether. Every move, and every failure to move, closes down the infinite range of possible worlds while opening up an entirely new range. And so, like my student, we sometimes freeze up. We don't want to regret our life, so we stop. But that doesn't really solve the problem: We're still responsible for stopping. I love the words of poet/teacher Peter Rollins: "There is then no way to escape the feeling of regret, except through fully embracing this experience of freedom."

So, Michael began to practice noticing his sensations and moods, acknowledging them, not judging them. With great patience, he allowed whatever was present to be as it was. He didn't build an identity out of any idea; he became willing to be present with, and let pass, both the great dramatic moments and the trivial, unattractive emotions. In this way, within a short time, Beginner's Mind gave him the life within his life back: real . . . and perfect.

meet there, in the suffering, the yearning, the commitment, the mystery.

But anyone who decides to take up Zen practice will need to connect with this deepest of intentions—though everyone will "say it" uniquely. Whether in the privacy of a can't-sleep night or entering a monastery and going in front of a guardian council, we have to get in touch with our clear intention to awaken. If all that is wanted is relief from mild stress, there are other ways that are perhaps better suited (I've been known to suggest getting a pet, relaxation techniques, even an occasional glass of wine . . .). It's only when you have decided that it is time to cut through the conditioning—everything sold to you by parents, teachers, peers, education, culture—and to stop living out of the program, responding like a robot, that Zen study can really begin. Then you will not be turned away from "the matter at hand." Why? Because underneath all the conditioning lives a person, and they are ready to begin peeling back all that conditioning and getting to, and living from, the ground of being.

Once that deep decision has happened, practice can begin to take genuine shape in your days. Your priorities shift, and then it's not quite as hard to change your schedule in accord with what's important to you. Meditation always "fits" into the hours of the day when you've become, gently and genuinely, unstoppable.

Sometimes a hero/shero helps. Mine for many years was the Buddha's stepmom, Mahaprajapati. She raised him, observed the devoted lives of the monastics who followed his teachings, and decided she wanted to do likewise. Being a man of his time, he said no. She shaved her head, donned simple robes, and followed him anyway, trekking hundreds of miles in bare feet. Over 500 other women saw her and followed her. (Some have called this "the first Women's March in the history of the world.") The Buddha, even seeing her bleeding feet, still said no to the women becoming part of the monastic community.

However we understand the patriarchy at play in this, let's focus just now on Mahaprajapati, how she kept practicing, stayed in the neighborhood, remained steadfastly committed to awakening. Eventually, an order of nuns was allowed to form (with some inarguably misogynistic rules added to their discipline). But she "persisted": She attended to the heart of things and led the other women in practice. Much has changed. Some things, of course, have not. In a hundred ways, we are each still called to access that "shero" within—to face our own challenges to realizing, practicing, and leading—and, like Mahaprajapati, to be unstoppable.

Meditation

Zazen, which is usually translated as *sitting Zen*, has always been the main practice of Zen. In centers, monasteries, and at home, students regularly get up around sunrise for zazen meditation and also end the day the same way. Many do retreats involving long hours of silent, seated, unmoving zazen. Zen, among all the schools of Buddhism, is the one that centrally emphasizes meditation practice, insight into the nature of things (Ch. *jianxing,* Jp. *kensho,* "perceiving the true nature"), and the personal expression of insight in daily life—specifically to benefit others.

Still, there is a great deal of misunderstanding about zazen. In contemporary usage, zazen is often lumped together with other methods from spiritual traditions that involve attaining

ALONE TOGETHER

We had just begun what would come to be known as "Cyber Monk," an online resource for those who could not come to group practice because they lived remotely or had other limiting circumstances. I was living in an A-frame on top of a mountain, doing a solitary retreat for three months, and my teacher said, "Myotai, you'll be the Cyber Monk. Help whoever writes get a practice together."

Most of those making contact in that initial period were young men playing around in the computer lab at college, just searching the web for something interesting and new, without any real interest in Zen. But then, one night, I got the first note from someone sincere and somewhat desperate:

"I live further out in the woods than you can imagine. There's really no chance I'll ever get to see a Zen teacher or community. Can you help me understand how to practice Zen? It's become the main thing for me. I don't want to just keep reading Zen books. . . . I feel so alone."

I looked around my lonely A-frame and realized how being on this solitary retreat had been forcing me to also find my "private practice" again, apart from the monastery. What had helped? What had been hardest? I began to share this with Izzy, and to hear about what she was facing, her victories and challenges. She and I would continue to correspond for years.

CONTINUED

I wrote her that I found it helpful to remember that Zen practice is fundamentally a solitary practice. The founder of Zen, Bodhidharma (ca. 440 to 528 CE), practiced alone for nine years in his cave. Zen did not develop into an organized group practice until the time of Daoxin (the Fourth Zen Patriarch), who created an intentional Zen practice community (ca. 630 CE). For the hundred or more years between Bodhidharma and Daoxin's intentional community, Zen remained the practice of scattered individuals and small groups of wandering ascetics. Izzy and I were in ancient, noble company.

Through the widespread development of Zen communities and monasteries, Zen practice often takes place as organized group practice. But solitary Zen practice has continued always—in fact, it is likely that unaffiliated and/or individual practitioners equal or exceed the number in organized groups, so we were also, though alone, part of a very big group.

We covered "the practicals" then (as we'll do in this book): where to practice, when to practice, how often to practice, how long to practice, what to practice, what to practice with. Sometimes we would agree to meditate at the same time. I'll always treasure her words: "Being alone-together with Cyber Monk gave me my practice." Being alone-together with Izzy had, in many ways, done the same for me.

some objective—a healthier or more peaceful mental/physical state, more harmonious social behavior, the resolution of this or that problem. While many meditation practices in the Buddhist tradition are helpful in achieving these things, zazen is ultimately a different animal.

Dogen (1200–1252 CE) was the founder of the Soto Zen tradition as well as a great mystic, poet, and meditation master. In Dogen's teachings, zazen is presented as "a wholly embodied posture." Most meditative traditions are somewhat dualistic: Practitioners initiate a method of meditation—counting breaths, visualizing sacred images, chanting, concentrating on an image or sensation—after establishing a seated position. This approach divides body-mind, makes them separate. Meditation is tacked on, added to body posture. Our seated posture, in dualistic meditation, is like the setting, and the meditating mind is the star of the show: The body sits and the mind concentrates.

Of course, when we're first receiving instruction on how to do zazen, we don't usually get it in one stroke. We initially take zazen apart into this piece and that piece, most often body, breath, and mind. Even Dogen wrote, "In our zazen, it is of primary importance to sit in the correct posture. Next, regulate the breath and calm down."

But after the preliminary stage, all instructions are integrated into one undivided whole: the body-mind of the practitioner of zazen.

All the capacities we usually make our identity with are let go for the period of sitting. We don't initiate movement, design anything to say, think anything through—we just sit. Since I work with people with quite varied physical capacities, old and young, conventionally abled and differently abled, I emphasize finding a comfortable relationship with gravity and then getting still. You don't have to be a flexible yogini to do zazen. Some folks will fold themselves into a cross-legged full lotus easily; others will position in their wheelchair, arrange pillows in their recovery bed, or need to accommodate knees that have climbed too many mountains. What helps is recognizing that the meditation won't be served by moving constantly in a search for a modicum of more comfort. We just need to settle the body and let it sit.

If zazen is not solving any problem, does it have value? Is purposeless activity good for anything? In one sense, entering zazen's non-duality allows us to take a break from using body and mind to get something or somewhere. Yet, even that description falls into a trap. As an old Zen koan says, "That's a good thing . . . but it's not as good as no-thing!"

How to Meditate

When it's the time when you want to meditate, usually a million other things will suddenly seem more important. So, the first step is simple and sometimes big: Just do it. Then, don't do something else . . . meditate. I've long coached students trying to get a practice started that it's helpful to decide on something so minimal that you can't talk yourself out of it. *I'll just go sit down for ten minutes*, or even, *I'll sit for ten seconds or so*. The important thing, as in so many things, is to just show up. Once you get to your sitting spot, you'll likely find it's enjoyable, or at the least that you actually end up staying a bit longer. But the first step is to just get in the neighborhood.

Decide on when. Set a time so that this becomes a routine, as much a part of your day as brushing your teeth. Consistency really helps. Also decide how long you'll meditate. Half an hour is usually good, but know yourself. Morning, before the agendas of work, etc., get started, is often a best time. (Try telling yourself as you're heading to sleep the night before that you're going to meditate in the morning. Put it in place in your heart-mind.) I've always liked sitting right before bed: It relaxes the muscles and helps with letting go of the day.

Find your spot. It is good to have a place set aside that you begin to associate with meditation. It can be a corner or a room. Keep your sitting pillow or chair there or nearby. Just seeing the space can remind you of your wish to integrate meditation into your life. *Why do I have that pillow in the corner? . . . Oh, right. . . .*

Enter consciously. Bring your hands together palm-to-palm at face-level for just a moment as you come to your seat. This is called *gassho,* and it's a physical gesture that means *two are being realized and practiced as one*—(so, in this case, your pillow or chair and you). Just this can shift consciousness. In Zen training, this gesture is used a great deal: We *gassho* to the room as we enter, to one another, to the altar, and even to the bathroom, and also when we arrive for a visit. In a sense, it's just a momentary pause, a chance to enter without judgment or a big agenda.

Establish your posture. It doesn't matter what you sit on, but it is important to be comfortable and stable. Try to create a good relationship with gravity, so your body doesn't strain with staying upright and balanced. (We'll look in chapter 3 at some of the postures that can help with this.)

Lower your gaze. It's helpful to keep your eyes slightly open; otherwise, sleepiness tends to be an issue. Then connect with your breath. Feel what your breath is doing: Just notice. You don't need to elongate it or change it in any way. Just be with it. . . . Many find it helpful to count with the breath for a while, as an assist to keeping attention focused there. As you exhale, count one; as you inhale, count two, and so on, up to ten. Then begin again at one. Anything we give attention to tends to deepen, and this will happen with the breath as well.

Return home. If you find your attention has shifted to some pattern of thought, notice it. Then, gently but firmly, let the thoughts go and bring your attention back to your breathing. (For instance, you remember you forgot to pick up your dry cleaning. Instead of just that thought, you build a whole thing: *What on earth will I wear to that meeting now? Why am I such a ditz? Mom never taught me how to be a grown-up. She's really. . . .*) Notice, acknowledge, return home to the breath. Begin the counting at one . . . (and leave poor Mom alone!).

Koans

When you hear stories about Zen, you often hear about koans (pronounced KO-ahns). Koans are the often cryptic and seemingly inscrutable questions or phrases used by Zen teachers to help clarify their students' understanding. Teachers often present

BEFRIENDING THOUGHT

Someone came to me to talk about how to begin meditation when she had chronic pain from a disease. She said when the pain was sharp, she was able to just experience what was happening without having an overriding sense of it being a problem. But when days of pain became persistent, she would often feel overcome with thoughts about how long it might last, whether she could bear it, what it meant about her future. She had a deep intention to see into the nature of reality and find peace but said she couldn't get past her physical and mental challenges. Her suffering was palpable.

We gently explored whether what she "knew" about the duration or significance of what was happening was certain, without any doubt. She actually smiled for the first time at that, as she acknowledged that what she'd become thoroughly convinced about wasn't the whole and complete truth. She had some facts, but she didn't really know her future, its every quality and possibility. Her anxiety had been coming in unbearable waves, and in the midst of it, she had been rocked off-center. Without denying her condition, she could also see that her opinions and ideas about it sometimes had a constricting effect, boxing her in.

We worked together on how to let her body and mind gently settle into sitting meditation. She reported that the anxious thoughts at first seemed to tumble in

CONTINUED

automatically, but then gradually seemed to slow down, and she could simply be with her breathing for longer and longer periods. I told her that even when she couldn't immediately let a train of thought pass, she might be able to just hang with it for a while, not ignoring it but also not giving the turmoil much energy, like you might with a child who was acting out. Holding thoughts gently like this, we usually see the energy drain from them naturally. As she quieted her mind, she noticed that she could actually see her fears as they arose, and instead of "building a world" out of them, she was increasingly able to let them continue down the stream of consciousness. This is not an easy practice by any means, and it was an honor to accompany her as she took up what many of us will do anything to avoid.

She, like most meditators, soon found that she was calmer and could feel her life more directly and honestly, both on the pillow and off. I was struck again by how quietly powerful it is to fully acknowledge and then release habitual patterns of thought. Even those that are "real issues"—like illness, grief, or deep concern about the state of the world—are helped when we practice and enable ourselves to be less distraught. Thoughts, it seems, are not so different from most people: They want to be acknowledged, and they grow calmer when met and recognized with genuine attention.

koans in formal talks (see the Dharma Talk section on page 115 for an example), and students may be asked to "realize" them in their meditation practice. Many koans can be traced back to the collections of sayings gathered by Chinese priests in the twelfth and thirteenth centuries. For example, one koan nearly everyone has heard of originated with Master Hakuin Ekaku: "Two hands clap and there is a sound; what is the sound of one hand?" Hakuin asked. The question often is abbreviated: "What is the sound of one hand clapping?"

All the koans are just ways of asking, *Who am I? What is reality?* They all address the ground of being, the nature of the self. By now, most of you probably know that the koan cannot be "resolved" through the intellect on its own; it is not a riddle. A clever answer won't put the question to rest. The question isn't intellectual, and neither is its resolution. Yet there is a resolution!

If we take up koan study too early in our practice, it can become just another intellectual exercise under the guise of Zen study, or what I often call "the definition of a waste of time." Koan study best happens under the guidance of a koan teacher who, by virtue of long experience, can assist in seeing what will best support your study. For those who cannot connect directly with a teacher, it can still be illuminating and inspiring to read or listen to koan-based Zen talks, which are now widely available.

If you're doing koan study, you enter into deep concentration, exhausting all discriminating thoughts . . . until a more intuitive realization arises. You then present your understanding of the koan to the teacher in a private interview called *sanzen*, or sometimes *dokusan*. The teacher may question to see if you truly have embodied the koan. When the teacher is satisfied that you've fully penetrated into it, she assigns you another koan.

If you have a koan teacher, it may indeed be helpful to do koan study. For some students, however, *shikantaza* (objectless meditation, or "just sitting") might be a more appropriate practice. Some students are more naturally attracted to koans. Their personality is always questioning, or the sense of repeated epiphanies deepens their spiritual life. Others are not. Their minds have a different quality, and to give them a koan to "work on" simply ties them in knots, seems irrelevant, and isn't helpful to them at all. One of my old teachers used to say, "Koan students come to enlightenment through huge, drenching thunderstorms. *Shikantaza* students are equally whetted by enlightenment, but their journey is through a gentle, steady rain." What is best may vary over the course of your study, with koans being helpful for a while and *shikantaza* then being more appropriate.

When a koan-trained teacher runs a Center, they will offer talks on koans regularly. These talks are always introduced as being "somewhat dark to the mind, but radiant to the heart," indicating that they are evocative and intuitive, and differ from expositions or explanations. Encouragement is given to "listen and receive" the dharma with "the heart not just the head."

Practicing a Koan

In Zen training, a koan would be given to you by a teacher only after your concentration has developed into *single-pointedness* (*joriki*), the falling away of self-consciousness. You would be provided private instruction and guidance in how to sit with your koan, release discriminating thoughts, and persevere until a more intuitive realization arises.

As mentioned, when you meet the teacher in dokusan and present your understanding, she may question to see if you have truly embodied the koan, and if not, send you back to work more deeply. When the teacher is satisfied that you have fully penetrated into the koan, she would then assign you another. If an intellectual presentation is made, rather than something direct, you will be sent back to your seat to go deeper.

It requires some trust and a willingness to persevere. Some students may work on one koan all their life; others will do hundreds. Koan study is one of the unique aspects of Zen study; it is rare when a tradition has anything like it for realizing one's true nature. It is somewhat of a trickster path, with the teacher evoking a clear presentation of what from the student's point of view can seem hopelessly elusive. When offered by a skilled and compassionate guide, koan study is also enormously generous and clarifying.

Just to give a flavor of what koan study might involve, here are a few of the initial "stopping koans" from the curriculum my students work with:

"How do you stop the fighting across the river?"

So, there is unrest. Maybe danger. By the time you get a boat and get over there, someone may have been hurt, or worse. Perhaps someone you love, your child, others who are really fragile or vulnerable. The situation is escalating. You can't just ignore it, and there's no one else to give the job to. It is "your business"—so tell me; show me: How do you stop the fighting across the river?

As you can see right away, this koan has application to our world, our relationship to every other being, and the suffering that is actively being enacted *right now*. It's a question about the nature of the self, and it presents an "impossible situation." To sit with and study this koan requires letting go of how we usually organize our self-idea. Who are you? Where are you? How does time function? Again, when taking up this koan, intimacy is required. We can't step back "out of the koan" an iota and actually resolve it.

What is it to *be the koan*, not just explain it, and "stop the fighting across the river"?

"Stop the ringing of the temple bell."

In this koan as well, we meet our world. Everything shouting, impinging, overlapping—beautiful sounds, screeching cars, sirens, mental chatter, poetry. The world is tearing into our private agenda, insisting that we show up, don't be late, answer the bells and whistles, solve seemingly critical problems, answer immediately when we don't have the answer. This koan may have been based in a monastery, where the bell rang to call everyone to meditation, dinner, work, or to present a koan to the teacher—but we all live in this koan.

"So, how do you stop the ringing of the temple bell?"

Again, don't put the koan outside your self.

To sit with the koan, you'll need to enter into an intense concentration, in which the koan is then brought up. A first step is to just repeat the words to yourself. In the atmosphere created by dropping into single-pointed concentration, the koan is experienced at a different level. A teacher will often instruct: "Don't separate your self from the koan!" to point the student away from objectifying and into their intuition. The words and meaning eventually dissolve and the koan is "seen through." Meeting with the teacher in private interview, you'd present your understanding. If an intellectual presentation is made, rather than something direct, the bell would be rung, sending you back to sit and go deeper. It requires a good deal of trust, in oneself and the teacher, to do this, as well as a willingness to keep coming back.

In my training, students did over 2,000 formal koans, working through many of the ancient collections. In koan study, an initial awakening *(kensho)* reveals the non-dual, but it is usually tentative, offering only the faintest glimmer. For most, habits will keep us acting and reacting pretty solidly from ego. The subsequent realizations and long, devoted practice after kensho helps to integrate our understanding into our daily lives. Koan study is powerful—explored with respect (and an adventuresome spirit!), it can profoundly change lives.

These are the most well-known collections of koans:

- *The Gateless Gate* (Japanese, *Mumonkan*), 48 koans compiled in 1228 by the Chinese monk Wu-men.

- *The Blue Cliff Record* (Japanese, *Hekiganroku*), 100 koans compiled in 1125 by Yuanwu Keqin.

- *The Book of Equanimity* (Japanese, *Shoyoroku*; sometimes called *The Book of Serenity*), 100 koans compiled by Master Wanshi Shokaku.

- *Mana Shobogenzo*, or the *300-Koan Shobogenzo*. Three volumes of 100 koans each compiled by Eihei Dogen. (1200–1253).

THE GREAT FOREST

A few years ago, I gave a talk about koan study in Black Mountain. Here is a brief excerpt:

Koan study is about suddenly illuminating where we live, seeing what is true about our lives, if only for a flash. Practice is the steady, ongoing living out of that truth.

Imagine you're a tree, whether you're planted in a parking lot or a deep woods, tall or small, tended or ignored, abused or the healthiest, best-loved tree in world. You are a tree, and you grow and thrive in accord with sunlight, moisture, weather, earth.

Suddenly there's an earth-penetrating flash: For just an instant, the light reveals that your roots are connected to every other tree, to every state, condition, time that trees have ever been. You get it: There is only one tree. It's completely natural; nothing has been changed or added. You're still planted uniquely right where you are as you are. But for a moment, it is clear for you in a way it never was before that you're also not separate, not alone, not confined. At once, it makes sense: If the tree down the road is getting rain, you're getting rain—because that tree is you. Harm to any tree harms you. The sense that another tree might crowd you, cheat you of light and nutrients, is obviously only one dimension of how it all works.

Though this is as real as bark and leaves, what you've seen may go dim in your awareness. The scene illuminated by that flash becomes somewhat of a memory. You feel alone and separate again. When your buds dry up because water has been diverted by someone's greed, you find anger arising. Though you've experienced what is real, you may still revert to a trance of separation, with fear and self-protection thickening up the bark, if you will.

This is the spiritual confusion ongoing koan study and practice directly address. Where do we live? We are here to help one another wake from our confusion and grow with dignity into this great, naturally compassionate forest of being. It's our real nature, our true home . . . and requires only that we not give up, on ourselves or any other being.

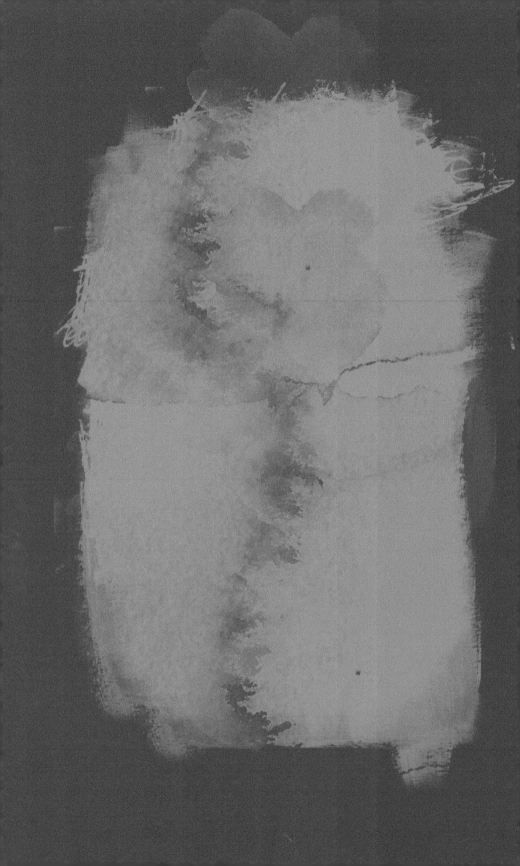

THREE

Sitting Zen

Zen begins with sitting down, dropping the masks, and entering into an intense, generous awareness.

Zazen literally means *seated Zen*. It is to stop running away, turning away, denying, making things up. It is the revolutionary gesture of sitting down and becoming quiet and still in the center of our life. It is seeing what that is when we're not pretending anymore. It is simple, honest, and sometimes quite raw. The posture of seated Zen embodies this . . . because if it's not embodied, it's still . . . just talk.

"Just sit," students will be told. All else will flow from that.

In a Zen monastery, the days and nights revolve around zazen, which is done in a large hall where everyone sits together for hours each day. At home, practitioners often begin and end each day in seated meditation: starting the day with awareness and letting go as the day concludes. Zazen is also understood to be a state of mind that penetrates all the other activities of our life—so work is zazen, eating is zazen, walking and talking are zazen. Indeed, if zazen doesn't penetrate daily life, we're quite likely misunderstanding it, using it "upside down," as an escape rather than awakening. (If we can sit with great composure but are content with being monsters biting everyone else's head off as soon as we stand up, then we've obviously missed the Zen bus.)

This is why one of the Three Treasures of practice is the noble community or sangha. The other two are Buddha and dharma. To become a Buddhist formally is to make vows to find refuge in the Three Treasures. Red Pine beautifully explained:

> *Taking refuge in the Buddha, we learn to transform anger into compassion; taking refuge in the Dharma, we learn to transform delusion into wisdom; taking refuge in the sangha, we learn to transform desire into generosity.*

—Red Pine, *The Heart Sutra: The Womb of Buddhas*

Though zazen is, in a sense, "an inside job," in that no one can do it for you, we also wake up together . . . or not at all. So, let's look into what it takes to establish a thoroughgoing sitting practice, at home as well as in group situations.

Beginning Instruction in Zazen

You arrive at the threshold, ready to begin.

What does it take? Put down the backpack. All the things you're carrying in: Set them down for a while. Trust that, for this, you don't need anything else. *This* is sufficient; you are sufficient to it.

Still, you need to show up. The ground of being isn't missing anything, but that only gets real in your life when you practice and realize it.

So, make space and time. *Gassho,* hands palm-to-palm, acknowledging that you are not apart from this room, not separate from this place you'll sit down in. It doesn't need to be different. You don't need to be different. There is enough time. You can hit a bell or singing bowl to begin, if you like. You can set a bell to ring after your meditation period, or light a 15- or 30-minute stick of incense.

Find your seat, your place of practice, maybe a *zafu* (sitting cushion) or comfortable chair. Find a seated posture that you know you can be relatively still in and not hurt yourself. Once you've settled your legs, open up your spine a bit by stretching upward and then relaxing, allowing your back to offer its full support. Tuck the chin in just a little, without leaning your head forward—this will help release neck tension. Press your tongue lightly against the upper palate; swallow gently, allowing your jaw to relax.

There's always a question of what to do with your hands. Solve it by forming the *cosmic mudra,* a hand position that supports meditation: Place your active hand palm-up, resting in your lap, your less-active hand on top of it, fingers overlapping. Allow the tips of your thumbs to just touch, as gently as you'd touch the cheek of a baby. You'll use that commitment to the thumbs gently touching to establish and maintain a state of mind.

If you begin to hold tension, the thumbs will likely press hard against one another. If you notice that, soften. If your mind begins to really wander, you may notice it first when you notice the thumbs have drifted apart. Bring them back together and gently come back into concentration. And if you get sleepy, you may notice it first when you become aware that your thumbs have drooped down as if to take a nap in your palm.

Reestablishing your hand position will help you wake up a bit. In this way, the mudra acts like a built-in "biofeedback device," supporting your intention to find a deeply relaxed, yet wakeful state of mind.

Now lower and soften your gaze, keeping your eyes still open slightly. Keeping the eyes open does two things: One, it breaks the chain of association that might otherwise lead you to fall asleep (which is what usually happens when we get quiet, become still, lower the lights, etc.). Two, it affirms that you're not "checking out": You're not putting cotton in your ears or closing your eyes. Instead, you're present, with your senses functioning, just without the customary commentary. Then, bring your attention to your breathing.

Zazen is this unadorned practice.

There may also be times when you want or need a guided meditation to jump-start your commitment. There are many apps and recordings that help in this way. See the Resources section (page 122) for suggestions.

Posture

Posture in zazen involves both the body and the mind. The *lotus position* (legs crossed onto opposite thighs) has been called the essence of zazen—in part because it is very stable and supportive, and perhaps also because the lotus thrives in a muddy pond, where otherwise stagnant waters blossom into astonishing, natural beauty. (My temple in NYC was called Fire Lotus to indicate that it was a place we'd use the fire and mud of daily life to fuel the flowering of spiritual life.) "No mud, no lotus," Thich Nhat Hanh famously said.

But the implication of the lotus as a way of understanding zazen isn't actually limited to those who, usually youngish and in the 20- to 40-year-old age range—or super-flexible yoga practitioners—can twist their legs into a pretzel shape. It is the radical stance of the mind and body in practice: Nothing is rejected; nothing better or other is needed.

The first key in seated Zen is to simply sit down; in other words, stop doing something else. Find a way of sitting that allows a sense of groundedness, stability, and comfort. This means: Establish a seated posture where you can be quite still for a good while without hurting yourself. Once you get settled, the practice does involve sitting still, essentially so we stop the internal habit of always "shopping" for some other position that is better than this. Most people find that, once they start that shopping, it is kind of endless: Adjust your foot, now your hip is out of line; move your hands a bit, suddenly your nose wants scratching . . . on and on. So, it's not about being rigid, just settling in.

If you can sit on the floor, use a pillow to raise your behind off the ground 3 to 4 inches. This helps create the slight curve natural to the lower back. Fold your legs so that one isn't pressing on top of the other, or else the bottom one will end up going to sleep as the minutes pass. Or sit on your knees using a bench or with a pillow between your legs. For a moment, elongate the spine a bit, and then relax, sway side to side a time or two, and you'll have opened up your vertebrae and hips and released any tension hiding there.

If you're better off in a chair, it's best to sit upright without leaning back into it—that usually creates an unnatural curvature, and in short order, it begins to ache. Instead, trust your spine and internal organs to do what they are designed to do:

support you. Keep your feet flat on the floor, or if you're shorter, on a pillow that lets you keep your feet flat. For bedbound practitioners, try to arrange some pillows to keep you as upright and supported as possible. If you're in a wheelchair, take a few moments to give attention to your posture and find your best alignment; placing a loosely rolled yoga mat vertically behind the spine can also be helpful.

Breathing

Once you've settled into a seated posture for zazen, it is time to bring attention to your breathing. The breath initially is used as a focus, an object of concentration. I always say it is the handiest focus possible, because if you're alive, you're breathing—you don't have to go get anything, like a candle, or remember anything, like a mantra. You simply bring your attention to your breath. Just notice what it's doing, where you feel it. That's it.

For many of us, the straightforwardness of this instruction is immensely challenging. We immediately start "messing with" the breath. We try to slow it, or deepen it, or whatever other idea we have about how it should be. But focusing on the breath in zazen is just that: feeling it as it is and letting it be. We're asked to make a commitment to the breath, not unlike the commitment we make to a deep friend: to notice, acknowledge, and not try to change. It's so simple, and can be so hard.

As I mentioned earlier, because this concentration on breath is not always easy, some teachers advise using a crutch for a while: Counting with the breath. With your exhale, count the number one. Inhale: two. Exhale: three . . . and so on up to the number ten, when you begin again at one. It can help to breathe into and out from the *hara*, the body's center of gravity, which is about two inches below the navel.

The only other agreement is that if you find yourself doing something else, acknowledge it and begin your counting at one again. Sometimes you'll catch yourself fairly quickly; other times you may find yourself quite well down the road chasing a train of thought—or up to number 200—before noticing. Sometimes it'll be just "brain popcorn," random thoughts that are relatively easy to release (think: song lyrics or a to-do list); sometimes it may be thoughts that seem profound, important. The practice is the same: The moment you notice yourself doing something other than counting the breath, gently acknowledge it, let it go, and return to your breath, beginning the counting with one.

Coming Home: Being Present

Once you've settled what you're doing with your legs and hands, established a supportive posture, and brought your attention to the breath . . . in one sense, you're home. There's nothing but deepening into zazen.

Still, during the first year or so of daily practice (and whenever you're particularly stirred up), you may face some common barriers. Many people report that they "never thought so much" as when they first sat down to meditate. Of course, what's really at play is attention: Ordinarily, we're not noticing what we might think of as the open faucet of thought. With zazen, we're waking up to it. Another common experience is thinking, *These thoughts shouldn't be happening; they're wrong.* But again, of course, the natural function of the brain is to think; it's as natural as your lungs breathing. What we're opening to is the possibility of not attaching to those thought patterns, passing feelings, or the meaning we add to various sensations.

For instance, various physical irritations and discomforts may come up. You've decided to settle in, be still, not chase, but a little drama may enter stage left. *I'll never walk again if I don't move right now.* or, *There's absolutely no reason not to scratch this itch; what is this, some kind of boot camp? I'm about freedom, dammit!* Just know that on the other side of the drama is a field of possibility we aren't so often acquainted with.

One of the great gifts of zazen is hidden in a bit of instruction: When a thought comes up, and no matter how many times you let it go, it returns and returns—that's the cue to shift your attention to that thought. Entirely. Utterly. Be it. So if the thought is *Sore shoulder! Sore shoulder!*—you give yourself to nothing but *Sore shoulder!* Not your thoughts *about* it, however, but with intimacy. Keep breathing into it until you become it so completely that there is no *you* looking at *it*. What most people find is that when that happens, the drama goes away. What had been unbearable . . . becomes simply a moment. This translates into a much less dramatic, much more generous life off the pillow as well.

Developing a Practice

Everyone's spiritual journey is theirs alone. What your particular background, body, emotional makeup, and "civilizational circumstance" enable will be completely personal. At the same time, people have been at this for a very long time. Here and there are bits of wisdom, the encouragement of inspiring words, the example of honorable, devoted, and compassionate lives.

The Buddhist tradition is a mixed bag of all these gifts, some useful, some not so much. There are incredibly inspiring teachers and teachings (as well as spectacular disappointments in character and compassion). For those who find themselves drawn to Zen training, it is important to exercise both a trusting heart and an ongoing discernment. There is, as always, a great deal of humanity in the mix—your own and that of all those around you. Gifts and curses, dragons and snakes, live together in this pond. Tread wakefully. But by all means, do tread!

There are all sorts of ways to develop a practice that really works for you. Let's briefly look at a few basics:

- **Make the space and time.** On a regular basis, at about the same time (or times) each day, sit down and meditate. Having a dedicated space is a reminder of this being a priority in your life, as will having a time you associate with meditation. Many find beginning and/or ending the day with meditation is helpful and can be worked in by getting up just a little earlier and/or including sitting as part of getting ready for bed. But also look at where in your life a meditation period fits best. Many young parents find that the best time is when their kids go down for a nap. Remember to start small: 10 to 15 minutes, so you don't talk yourself out of it too easily.

- **Practice where you can.** Meditation is wonderfully portable: It goes where you go and can be engaged at any moment. The train ride home. The waiting room at the doctor's office. My NYC students did "elevator meditation": when the elevator bell rang as they went up or down, they used that as a meditation gong, calling them to come back to their breath.

- **Practice with others.** It can be very encouraging to sometimes sit with others, which we'll discuss more, and there are many opportunities now to join others at Zen centers, monasteries, and evening sitting groups, as well as longer retreats.

Individual Practice

There's no place like home. One of the reasons it's nice to have a home practice, rather than just going on retreats, is that it guards against our habit of dividing our life. We're less likely to develop a "Zen center persona" that is smooth and peaceful, who is perhaps altogether different from who we are at home. It is possible to engage "work practice" and "dish duty" mindfully at the center but still maintain a household reputation for never washing your cup, etc. Making your home your "temple of practice" helps us see the sacred in the mundane, right where we live.

Just like you have to go through having the flu with a lover to really know them, you have to go through some weather with your spiritual practice, too. When you live with your practice, through the highs—the times of great determination and the spiritual romance—as well as through the lows—the grubby and grumpy days and the times of pervasive doubt—it begins to get very stable. You begin to show up with a deep honesty and humility, no matter what is going on.

As you begin to establish this commitment to show up, to sit and practice your life, regardless of mood or whatever challenges are at play, a shift happens. It truly becomes your own, for one thing, and you become less vulnerable to the shifting winds, the opinions and attitudes of others who may or may not love that you're giving time to what might look to them like useless "staring at your navel for hours." (Though I've also heard from plenty of spouses of practitioners who love how their mate comes home from retreat, or what even a single sitting period can do to ease the tension that had been between them.)

You become less vulnerable as well to "the meanie" who may have held sway in your mind, with habitual judging and belittling your every effort. The practice of acknowledging and letting go can take the power away from that voice.

Those with a strong individual practice also find that they're often more flexible in their perspective. A capacity to enter other points of view and to intuit and respect others' experiences is part of the practice. This makes relationships a good deal richer and infuses them with natural kindness.

Group Practice

The emphasis in these pages is to provide you with what you need to establish a daily practice. But Zen is not just a solitary spiritual practice. Sitting, studying, and talking with other practitioners, working together side by side—all these are integral to the life of Zen. So, I encourage you, if possible, to make a commitment to sit with other people, too. In the United States, there are now hundreds of Zen meditation centers and sitting groups, as well as other kinds of Buddhist meditation groups. The online world of Zen is percolating as well—you can listen to dharma talks by teachers and join discussion groups with other students. (See the Dharma Talk at the back of this book, page 115, as well as the Resources section, page 122, for books, apps, and meditation centers.)

BOWING IN

At the beginning of a sitting period, it is traditional to bow to an altar, offer a stick of incense, and bow once more. Then, as you stand before your seat, bow toward and away from your cushion, bench, or chair. Each of these gestures helps us enter meditation intentionally. If you are new to using incense as part of meditation, it is offered to indicate that this session is for all beings, not just for oneself. If incense is not something you want to use (if you have allergies, for instance), you might try placing a small bowl of water on your altar for the same purpose, refreshing it regularly. An altar is simply the little table where you place objects that remind you of your spiritual intention. Some people like to place an image of the seated Buddha or a standing bodhisattva (compassionate being) with a candle and a flower in a vase.

The standing bow to and away from our cushion expresses respect for our practice and for those—whether present or not—who practice with us. In other words, we acknowledge that, though we are sitting by ourselves, we are not alone.

Community is sometimes likened to a rock polisher: Students bump into one another, help work off the rough edges, and shine each other up a bit. It can actually be easy, given some quiet time to chill, to convince oneself, *I'm awake; no problems left here.* That attitude—developed in solitude, usually with no opportunity for awareness of the inevitable problems we're causing left and right—depends on interaction for "remedy." It's just hard to see alone when we've got a bad case of "Zen stink"—many varieties exist; all have a scent of being full of oneself but calling it dharma. A teacher and a community tends to clear this from the system pretty quickly. Equally easily, too much time in solitude can allow us to exercise a habit of negative self-talk. Community can be a wonderful place to see that we're just an ordinary human and that our life and practice are okay, even appreciated. There is a reason that Zen centers often chant, "May we realize the Buddha Way together."

Also know there is no need to be nervous about the protocol when you come to group meditation. When you arrive, simply keep your eyes and ears open, and you'll be guided by the situation or by one of the more senior students. Usually there is a place to take off your shoes, and then there is a small bow from the waist as you enter. When you get to your seat, you bow to it and then to the people across the room from you. This small gesture of bowing the head indicates that we're arriving with respect and offering our practice in support of one another.

DISCARD THE EXTRA

It was 1987.

Me: *"Why are all the Zen teachers' names we recite men? Where are the women in Zen history? Why are the statues and paintings depicting the spiritual path in the monastery all male figures?"*

My teacher: *"You'll change this when you are a teacher. For now, just sit."*

Me: *"But . . ."*

Much of my own training was in a center led by an Italian American man who had received authority to teach from a Japanese man. My teacher held a deep commitment to develop an American monasticism for those called to train as monks or nuns, as well as to create a dynamic lay training for those "in the world." I did ordain as a monastic, shaved my head, and lived a life of service, with vows of poverty and selflessness, for over two decades of my adult life. The program of training, with a residential community and thousands of lay students joining for retreats and short-term residency, was a tremendous gift.

There were also significant issues and challenges at the center, in part due to the combination of two powerfully patriarchal cultures being so heavily in the mix. And I am a woman, have worked for women's empowerment all my life, know the patriarchy to be incredibly harmful, and had left the Episcopal Church of my youth when the priest told me my brother could be an altar boy, but girls weren't allowed up there. (I remember joking that if they'd met *my* rascal brother, this rule would have been reconsidered much earlier on!)

So, when I began teaching many years later, though things had improved a little, I needed to find a way forward that spoke powerfully to the issues I'd encountered, as well as to the depth of gratitude and obligation I will forever have to and for my teachers.

> *Learn the rules like a pro, so you can break*
> *them like an artist.*
> —Pablo Picasso

Perhaps it is so for all students: Find what is useful/clarifying, open to not knowing; discard what is extra. Repeat ad infinitum. That is the basic, and in some ways the most demanding, imperative of Zen practice—ongoing awakening and making the way a little clearer for others when we can.

THE VOICE OF THE BUDDHA

Many groups that meet for Zen practice will include a chanting service. This can involve a recitation of a Zen teaching or a rhythmic style of chanting with the accompaniment of instruments. Sometimes the words will be translated into English, and sometimes they will be in another language (my temple, for instance, sometimes chanted in Japanese).

You may find this a little shocking, especially if you've never experienced anything like it before. We also may expect Zen to be free of ritual or "religious" overtones, so it's helpful to see how chanting with a group can genuinely be supportive. Be open to the experience, and see for yourself.

Chanting is a form of meditation—we breathe, produce sound, and attune to the voices around us. Sometimes the words will just wash over you, filling you. Other times, the discriminating mind will keep questioning. Each time that happens, the practice is to return to the sound and put your self in unity with the community. Zazen practice tends to be solitary, even when we do it within sangha. Chanting is something practiced together—hearing one another, giving voice together, moving in concert.

Chanting is also an expression of gratitude: A typical part of a chanting service is a list of Buddhist teachers from the time of Shakyamuni Buddha 2,500 years ago up until the present day. This is also a chance to call to mind the people who have taught and supported you, to whom you feel gratitude.

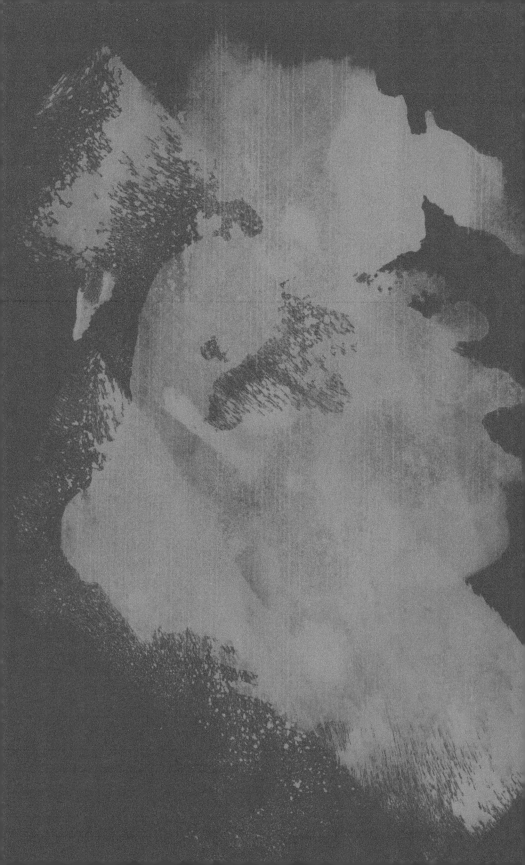

FOUR

Moving Zen

We all know the thud of returning from vacation: We've had a bit of time released from the constraints of work commitments, and suddenly we're back home and need to show up at particular times for particular things, solve problems, deal with "the whole catastrophe." The time away may be wonderful, but it also feels distinctly other than our daily life. It is possible to have our Zen practice exist solely in this way, too, like a vacation or time away from our "real life." But it is also possible to have a Zen practice that includes our life away from the cushion: working Zen, talking Zen, relationship Zen, etc. When we move, our practice moves. It is when that possibility is engaged that lives begin to change.

How so? For one thing, we tend to stop defining ourselves as victims. We also find it easier to drop the hero act. We come to a basic sense of responsibility for this life by noticing its basic nature and inherent interconnectedness. Life begins to open up in a way that is more integrated, more open, touched with both natural humility and natural confidence. Every time a practitioner *practices*, fear is lessened, arrogance is less likely, and a door opens to compassionate activity. It is truly that significant a shift for a human being to genuinely practice moment by moment. We shouldn't underestimate the power of practice, especially consistent, day-by-day, whatever-the-weather practice.

The 90-year-old Pablo Casals, the world-famous cellist/composer/conductor, asked why he still practiced eight hours a day, said, "Because I think I'm beginning to make some progress."

You can get a glimpse of "all things are one" and still be quite a creep and do others all sorts of harm . . . if you don't practice. We can realize "everything is interconnected" and still destroy the ecosystem, or violate someone sexually . . . if we're not practicing. And we also *can* practice any aspect or moment of our day. We'll need to "turn the light inward" and examine our habits, privileges, and attitudes, so that we can interact without bias or presumption.

Let's look at some of the areas where practice can come to life.

Stop Shopping for a Better Moment

Zen practice asks us first to sit down. Physically, emotionally, and spiritually, we're asked to *just sit*. In other words, through literally taking our seat, we stop the habit of shopping for a better moment, a better place, something other than what is *right here*. Only when we do that can practice begin to enter our lives moment by moment. Until we do that, we're still shopping. The radical simplicity of sitting embodies a truth, a sufficiency that most of us find hard to believe. We'll argue it to death: *But aren't I supposed to try harder?* For now, just sit. *But what about everything else?* Just sit. If you really sit, you'll find you're sitting when you stand, work, advocate, love, and work. But for now, just sit. *What does that mean, "Just sit"?* You know.

So, you sit down, ten minutes, or half an hour, maybe several short periods, maybe morning, then morning and evening. The sitting body will let you know when it requires a bathroom break or a stretch. You find some days there is a good deal of mental activity to notice, many thoughts coming and going. Other days are quieter, or even groggy. One day your shoulder aches a bit, and instead of shifting, you see that it's okay, no harm done by sitting through it. Another morning, you're getting a cold and shorten the period, sensing you need more sleep to get well. There's the month when your foot is in a cast from tripping in the parking lot, so you sit in a chair instead of on your favored pillow. Your seated meditation becomes something you just show up for, not unlike brushing your teeth. It's not a big deal, but part of how you live in a healthy way.

Still, at some point it is time to stand up: At once, you're at a threshold. How will practice walk with you into your day? How can some of this inner stillness be found when we're engaged in the "ten thousand things"? Years ago, I developed a series of inner chants called the Seven Thresholds to help my students mark these liminal moments with a mind of practice. We'll explore them in this and the next chapter.

Try this first one: It can be a "first thought of the day" or used following morning meditation. Repeat silently three times:

> *This day of being blessed by blessing*
> *being honored by honoring*
> *being love by loving, I awaken.*

—from the Seven Thresholds

Mindful Walking

What makes walking into a practice is one shift: It is not about going somewhere; it is about *being* somewhere. Just be in the step, not down the road or off in the clouds. And when your attention wanders or becomes attached to a destination: notice. Then gently bring your attention back.

Walking meditation is one of the most natural practices we can develop—it will help us feel calmer, more connected to place, and generally more aware. When it's done in a meditation hall with others (this is called *kinhin*), instructions are given that guide everyone on how to walk in harmony with one another. Kinhin in the meditation hall quietly bonds the group. It also prevents the meditative state from becoming associated with only one position (and it gives the knees a little break).

Walking practice also connects us to our life. How many times have you trekked for some distance, only to realize you didn't notice anything at all about the journey? You missed the store, the bird, the cloud. You didn't hear the music, didn't register the rain. Thoreau bemoaned this, and called us to let our feet awaken the world a bit:

> *I am alarmed when it happens that I have walked a mile into the woods bodily, without getting there in spirit.*

> —Henry David Thoreau, *Walking*

Just as seated Zen is sometimes called "the noble posture," walking Zen also has a sense of ease and dignity, as if you were a king or queen slowly meandering on a royal stroll. Thoreau might have called this *sauntering*. At home, you only need a short hallway, and there won't be as many distractions as there are outside.

You can, however, make walking a practice whenever it's time to head down the street, or to and from the subway or your car. Sometimes I suggest this as stealth *kinhin*. No one needs to know you're "doing a practice"—just walk and stay in the moment. (Remember, though, that it's good not to "walk around like zombies," in some exaggeratedly slow manner while out in public!) Just relax, enjoy walking for its own sake, and instead of the habitual planning and thinking—actually feel the sensation of your foot hitting the ground.

When you find your thoughts have wandered and you're a million miles away, exhale and let go, and see if you can return to the sensation happening at that moment, with your step bringing you back to exactly and perfectly *here*.

Mindful Eating

In a Zen monastery, at least one meal a day is served and received in a ceremony called *oryoki*. The meal is taken in the meditation hall, largely in silence, with each student using a shiny set of black nested bowls. (One of my teachers who'd been in the Navy called these the Zen Mess Kit.) It's actually one of the more elaborate ceremonies in Zen training, with drumrolls, the striking of clappers, and an offering taken slowly up to an altar. It's almost as if, even in ancient times, it was clear that it can take a big bang of the "mindfulness drum" to slow down and recognize that each meal we're taking part in is a miracle of sorts.

Oryoki means *just the right amount*. The instruction is to not eat so much that your meditation becomes groggy, yet

IN EACH STEP

One way to integrate your practice into your life is to practice the transitions from one posture to another. If you've been doing seated practice, for instance, when it is time to stand up, do your best to stay in the meditative mindset. Get up gently, getting your feet under you solidly, without engaging a lot of interior dialogue. Bow to your seat, allowing gratitude for the opportunity to meditate to express itself.

Select a quiet place where you can walk at ease, indoors or out. You only need to be able to take somewhere between ten and thirty paces, and then turn and come back to where you started, making that circle for ten or so minutes. Let your hands rest easily, held at your waist. (The left hand creates a fist with the thumb tucked inside, and the right hand covers the left hand. Be sure to keep your shoulders relaxed.)

Feel the ground through the bottoms of your feet, as well as the other somatic sensations that come along with a standing posture. Keeping your eyes lowered a bit, take small, slow steps. It can help to link the walking to the breath: inhale, exhale, move one foot forward half the length of the other foot, repeat. After a few minutes of establishing your concentration with slow walking, you can speed it up to a normal walking pace.

As with the breath in sitting, your attention will wander away many times. As soon as you notice this, return attention to the feel of the next step. In meditation halls, walking meditation happens for about ten minutes in between longer sitting periods. (This is also the time people leave to use the bathroom if they need to.) At home, you may want to do likewise, putting a five- to ten-minute walk between thirty-minute periods of meditation. When you're ready to sit down again, bow to your seat and reestablish your sitting posture.

enough to remain healthy. There are a few chants that are part of the ceremony, calling attention to all those who worked on our behalf so that we can receive food in our bowls. There is a moment when everyone together chants a vow to keep that kindness going forward.

One of my Zen friends, teacher Jan Bays, commented beautifully:

> When we are able to fully appreciate the basic activities of eating and drinking, we discover an ancient secret, the secret of how to become content and at ease. . . . I didn't understand "right amount" very well until I began practicing mindful eating. I saw that mindful eating is ethical action. It is ethical action toward our self, toward all the beings who bring us our food, and toward all those who are hungry in the rest of the world.
>
> —Jan Bays, *Mindful Eating: A Guide to Rediscovering a Healthy and Joyful Relationship with Food*

Getting tuned into "just the right amount" is a practice, both in the meditation hall and more generally as we study our habits around hunger, satisfaction, greed, and self-absorption.

Mindful Working

We can practice our livelihood in any number of ways. We can see it as just doing a job, rounding up the money we need, or a way to pass the time and not be bored. We may be so passionate about our work that the rest of our lives dims in importance. But work can also be seen in a different light altogether—as a fundamentally sacred activity. This is why Layman P'ang (who often appears in koan collections) once said, "Isn't it wonderful? Isn't it marvelous? I chop wood and carry water."

In order to shine that light on work, practice involves examining our habits, the ways we approach things. It's like the old story of the three masons working on a cathedral: Asked what he was doing, the first mason muttered, "I'm hammering this stupid rock, and I can't wait 'til 5 when I can go home." The second mason, asked the same question, sighed with overwhelming boredom and said, "Well, I'm molding this block of rock so that it can be used with others to construct a wall. It's not bad work, but it's just the same exact thing, day after day." The third, with a lively spark in his eye, responded, "Well, kind sir, as you can see, I am building a Sacred Temple!"

So, how we see a thing can actually change what that thing is. But how do we make every day a "Bring Your Practice to Work Day" and manifest this transformative potential? First, do your best to find work that does no harm. It can also help to begin each day with another of the Seven Thresholds, recited internally a time or three:

Not knowing the full outcome of my effort
I will be generous, resilient, and creative in my service
And work to benefit life and relieve suffering

—from the Seven Thresholds

Let arriving at your desk or place behind the counter begin with this small, still-the-mind pause. Breathe. Then, as you take up whatever "ax and pail" you use to chop the wood and carry the water of your tasks, both you and they are transformed. Our job description does not define our real work, which is much deeper. We are here to make a place that awakens, a

MEALS AS MEDITATION

Here are two practices for stealth *oryoki*, ways of receiving a meal in daily life in an awakened way, one for when eating out at a restaurant and one for when at home.

Recite aloud or silently:

> *The undivided life of all beings*
> *I vow to taste, appreciate, and continue it*
> *with wisdom and compassion*
> —from the Seven Thresholds

Restaurant Practice

1. After reciting the chant to yourself, do a quick inner-outer scan:
   - Notice your basic hunger and thirst level; remember when you last ate or drank water.
   - Note what activities (energy demands) you've been engaged in and will be moving into after the meal.
   - Acknowledge whether anything emotionally challenging might impact how you interpret what nourishment you need.
   - Read the room: Is it calm or frenzied?

2. When your waitstaff arrives, register that they are helping you and will bring you, literally, the gift of life.
   - None of us earn this; not everyone receives it, even when they need it.
   - Tell them clearly, with consideration for their service, what you would like for your meal.

3. When your food arrives, say thank you.
   - Say this genuinely to whomever brings your meal.
   - Let thankfulness spread in your mind and body. So many things and people have given of themselves to bring this to you. The sun shone; the rain fell; the farmer labored; the trucker trekked; the grocer, baker, and cook did their work. Without your earning any of it, all of it is in your bowl, fills your cup, will feed your cells, give you strength, and become whatever you create. Time to notice.

4. Taste and enjoy. Make the quiet promise again to continue the generosity you've received. (Beginning with a good tip is nice!)

Home Practice

1. Designate one special bowl that you'll use for meals when you are doing stealth *oryoki*. I give each of my students a beautiful wooden Just-the-Right-Amount bowl wrapped in a cloth for this purpose. The purpose of having a designated "practice bowl" is just to stop the flow of habit a bit; it functions to remind us to pay attention. (See Resources, page 122, if you'd like to receive a bowl from Hermitage Heart.)

2. Recite the Inner Meal chant to yourself.

CONTINUED

3. Prepare your food mindfully; let your senses awaken to smells, tastes, textures, colors. Slow down; cook in silence hearing the sounds of chopping, sizzling, etc.

4. Prepare your mind by calling to presence all the beings that contributed to your receiving this food. Go wide. . . .

5. Eat silently. Allow yourself to just eat, not make a lot of internal commentary. (If you don't live alone, you can also practice "stealth *oryoki*": Use your designated bowl, and include the company at the table in your practice of gratitude by engaging with them in loving, attentive conversation. You can also explain to your kids that sometimes when you want to eat quietly and really taste your food, you use your Just-the-Right-Amount bowl and it helps the food taste even better. Sometimes they will want a special bowl for themselves, too.)

6. When you're done, mindfully clean your bowl.

Sacred Temple, gesture by gesture. And when we find we've done something else . . . to acknowledge that, and begin again.

Mindful Moving

When Siddhartha Gautama was early on in his search, he tried various practices of extreme physical denial: He excelled at the yogic disciplines, fasting for long periods, not sleeping, etc. He became "the skinniest of the skinny," fasting longer and more severely than anyone else. But he found that not only did none of these disciplines ultimately serve the purpose of awakening, they were completely wrongheaded. A pivotal moment in the telling of the Buddha's story is when he accepted sweet milk from a kind woman, Sujata, and recovered his strength. (Perhaps a woman-honoring retelling of this story is due, one that credits her with a body-wise spiritual teaching, served up alongside his dipper of milk.)

All to say: The Buddha realized that our physical bodies are the location of our practice and awakening. If we're not respecting the wisdom of our bodies, we're outside of wisdom. In Zen practice, we are taught to neither deny our sensations nor to make a particularly big deal of them. Zazen does this when it asks that we embody stillness, letting the attention settle along with the nervous system. Even as deep meditative states develop, during which all self-consciousness is released and "body and mind fall away," students will eventually need to get their feet back under them and walk about in the world. It helps to set up some ways to rejuvenate your practice throughout the day, as the sweet milk Sujata served up did. Here's one way that

ONE JOB

There are many of us who feel that our shared work right now is brought into clear focus by the gravest crisis ever to face the human race: the disruption of our planetary climate and the threats posed by that to civilization and sentient life. Regardless of profession, stage of life, or age, we all have this one job. According to the United Nations Intergovernmental Panel on Climate Change (IPCC), the next ten years or so will determine everything, and there is already no way to avoid the consequences of not having done the work earlier. Entire countries and communities are suffering; inaction means ever more dire and wide-spread destruction.

To practice this work requires showing up, as all work does. To practice this work requires that we acknowledge failure, grieve honestly, and build resilience. On any given day, our work will be thunderously inadequate. We may hunger for distraction, fall into anger, forget what is at stake.

So how do we find our individual practice in this monumental work?

Start. Do at least one thing every day that brings the truth of "addressing climate disruption is my work" into active expression.

Company presidents will have different tasks than adolescents. Journalists will do what retired elders can't do, and vice versa. Your "one thing" may become many things . . . or morph into another unanticipated thing altogether.

But do one thing.

A Few Ideas for Getting Started

- Speak out for change and vote for climate-informed representation; reduce and reuse before recycling; green your commute (public transit, biking, car sharing, flying only when absolutely required); review and reduce home energy use (use cold water to wash clothes, winterize, unplug); eat meat-free and don't waste; divest from fossil fuels (work to change how your workplace, pension, or university invests); arrange to offset your own carbon use through the UN's climateneutral.now.org.

- When you forget, and notice, just start again. I've often noted, "It's amazing how long it takes to do something when you never get started!" Keep starting. That's the magic.

- Use your rage—whether in reaction to social injustice, to our leaders' insanity, or to those who threaten or harm us. Rage is a powerful energy that, with diligent practice, can become transformed into fierce compassion. When you find your emotions rising, don't deny them, but recognize that they are inviting you to get creative, to use your imagination and intelligence on behalf of life. Let that energy challenge you to find ways to serve, protect, and create new possibilities.

wakes up gratitude (and also reminds you to stay hydrated and healthy!).

Repeat silently as you drink each of 4 to 5 glasses of water during the day:

One taste, one life
this ordinary tap water
impossible to earn
—from the Seven Thresholds

Body practice includes not only mindful exercise, but also our encounter with the various, often difficult, sensations of old age, sickness, and dying. My students with chronic illness, those who are differently abled, and home-bound elders have some of the deepest and most profound body practices. They teach me about the unstoppable, and the exquisitely ordinary, again and again.

Resting Meditation

We are a chronically exhausted culture. Ask just about anyone, and they'll be able to recount how few hours of sleep they're getting, how frenzied their schedule is, how overwhelmed they are with the complexity of their lives and the enormity of issues at play in the world.

There has always been what the Buddha diagnosed as "the fundamental unsatisfactoriness of conditioned existence" (*dukkha*, the First Noble Truth). But now there are increasingly well-crafted technologies designed specifically to shift our attention toward wildly tempting pits of distraction. Each

SEEING BEYOND THE BARRIER

Let's look at a body practice you can do with a friend. First, though, especially if you tend to be a solitary type, here's another chant that can open the heart to practicing with others:

Repeat silently as you prepare to meet someone:

The myriad ocean waves
each distinct and perfect
I meet myself in every being
—from the Seven Thresholds

A Body Practice Exercise with a Friend

Sometimes there are things we can't see without a friend to practice with. This is one reason we *gassho*, greet with respect, when we meet other practitioners. In this exercise, you'll help another work with how they encounter barriers.

- Stand facing a wall, between six and eight feet from it. Plant your feet solidly about a foot apart. Flex your knees slightly and center your balance in your lower abdomen. Relax your arms and shoulders, letting your hands rest at your sides. Lower your gaze, and spend a minute or two focusing on the movement of your breath.

CONTINUED

- Your partner should stand about a foot closer to the wall, their left shoulder perpendicular to your right. When both of you are in place and concentrating, they should then solidly extend their dominant arm out in front of you, forming a barrier, and command, "Try to get through my arm!"

- Open your eyes and walk forward, attempting to break through the barrier of their arm.

- Note (and enjoy) the experience.

- Reset into your original positions. Do your breathing practice for several minutes.

- Your partner should extend their arm solidly in front of you again, but this time instruct you, "Open your eyes, and walk toward the wall with everything you've got. Get to the wall!"

- Open your eyes and walk forcefully to the wall, your attention completely and utterly on the wall.

- Note the experience.

Was there a difference? Almost everyone seems to find that when they concentrate on the barrier, it stops them. When they put their attention on the wall, the next thing they know, they're there!

promises deliverance from loneliness and lack; all fail to deliver on the promise. Still, we're up late searching the web, mindlessly, looking for likes, looking for anything that answers the question we can barely express. We have access to more entertainment and information than any generation in history. Parents often have less support than ever in the demanding work of making human beings; the village, if there at all, is busy with its own agendas. And workplaces have increasingly little emphasis on the rights that guarantee a living wage or decent hours.

Because of this, having a commitment to practice rest is an imperative part of Zen practice. Ancient Buddhist teachings have thousands of words on the dangers of sloth and torpor; my sense is that modern students need more encouragement at the other end of the continuum. And so the question: How can we include deep sleep and profound rest in our Zen practice? I like it when my students aren't nodding off in the Meditation Hall, but I don't want them swigging gallons of coffee to get there.

Two of the Seven Thresholds speak to creating this symbiotic relationship between resting and activity. The first is a practice of pausing at twilight, becoming aware and still for a moment, and entering the evening hours consciously. As simple as it is, students report that it makes a tremendous difference.

Sundown (recite silently):

> *Daylight ends;*
> *darkness removes all difference*
> *Exhaling, I am at ease*
> —from the Seven Thresholds

Perhaps it's that whenever we exhale, our body does relax a bit, so it's just a nice thing to remember to do. Maybe it's that it quiets that background tension of *Your days are numbered!* and allows a moment of *This changing light is beautiful.* We stop being afraid of the dark at that moment. We rest, for a few breaths, in ourselves and the wholeness of life's process.

LET THE BABY SLEEP

I remember a number of years ago, sitting down at an NYC restaurant table to share a meal with a student who'd requested time together. It was in the early days of cell-phones being with everyone everywhere all the time, so it was still striking when she put her phone beside her on the table. While she was talking, her eyes would drift down to the phone, checking in on its little beeps and twitterpa-tions. It was like being with someone with a newborn. I didn't doubt that she really wanted to talk with me, but there was a "crying baby" demanding attention sitting between us.

She'd begin to open up about serious issues going on in her family and work life and then lose the track. She was eating the food we were brought—but again, like a new mom, distractedly, because job one was feeding the equiv-alent of a cranky baby-phone attention when it cried.

I said, "I think you might need to come talk with me sometime when you can be without your phone, don't you think?" She immediately put the phone on sleep mode, put it away, and made apologies. As we talked about the chal-lenges in her life, she realized that what she needed to do more generally was exactly what she'd done at our table. To be more present with the people she loved and to do the work she felt so lucky to do, she needed to put the baby-phone down for naps . . . and let her distractions rest.

So, since none of us are immune from "screen preoccu-pation," it is good to have some practices to shift toward

CONTINUED

another possibility. Know that for most of us, this is not an easy corner to turn. A few ideas:

Just like in a theater, practice turning your phone completely off when you are having a meal or conversation. For that hour or so, just be with the person you're with, the food you're being served. And don't worry; it is highly unlikely you'll forget to turn it back on. Try doing the same thing for time alone with yourself. Turn your phone completely off (or leave it at home), and go shopping, go for a walk, or read a book. Befriend your mind. And as bedtime approaches, power everything down an hour or so ahead of lights-out. I keep a timer set to remind me to do this. Voilà: There's a perfect bit of "real estate" opened up for meditation.

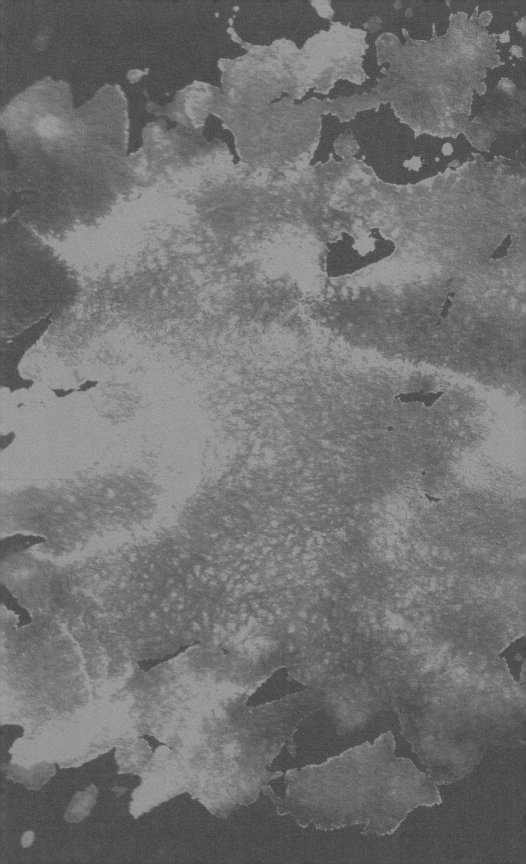

FIVE

Waking Up

Awakening is not a thing; it isn't a thought or an experience. It is noticing what is and that there is no solid line between you and all other beings, things, and conditions. Sometimes this is referred to as the "intimacy" of awakening: It is closer than close, because there is nothing outside or other. Words fail a bit here, since they are descriptions.

The first time this happens it can be somewhat dramatic, but in practice it continues, again and again and again, usually quite undramatically. There is a flavor to Zen's traditional descriptions of awakening that can make it seem like a big thing happens, and that changes everything forever. In one way, this is true, of course. It's a little like having the light flicked on in a dark and unfamiliar room. You see what's here clearly, and you can't go back to the same assumptions and fears.

But there is also no steady state—absolutely everything is impermanent, even insight. So, there's no "special" place you occupy once that insight has happened, where peace is forever and you make no further errors. (In other words, there's no magical escape to a place your poop doesn't smell.) This is the spirit of a lovely, almost funny saying, paraphrasing the great thirteenth-century master, Eihei Dogen, "It is all one continuous mistake." He also encouraged "ceaseless practice," which is kind of the checkmate to being stuck in those mistakes.

Barry Magid, an NYC Zen teacher, has aptly said, "Awakening is the progressive—or sudden—loss of one fantasy after another (including) of 'awakening'—until one is left with one's ordinary mind, just as it is, with no self-centered project of becoming more or other than who one is in the moment." I would add a caution: The next fantasy will always arrive. That's how the mind works. To meet that arrival, acknowledge it, and let it go is to practice our lives.

Words you will encounter in Zen's teaching on enlightenment: *kensho*, which means *to see*, and the related term, *satori*, which means *to know*—both point to this dropping away of the self, the trance, and imply a transformative opening of heart and mind. Still, when there is real awakening, in a very real sense there is no one "there" to know or see that the "self is forgotten."

Enlightenment doesn't change someone into a super-special person. In fact, if some deeply moving spiritual experience has left you feeling kind of special, in all likelihood you're miles from enlightenment. There are few things less pleasurable than hanging out with someone convinced that they are an enlightened being . . . while they basically ignore how asleep at the wheel they are!

Let's explore some techniques, practices, and forms that may assist in developing that "ceaseless practice" that Dogen referred to.

The Zen Way

One key to beginning to take up our lives in a Zen way is to appreciate what the teachings call the *absolute* and the *relative*. There's a great deal of discussion in the teachings about these two aspects of reality and how it's important not to get "stuck" in one or the other, and sometimes it can all get pretty philosophical and abstract. But let's see what's really at play, encounter it with our "beginner's mind," and see what might be helpful.

The relative: the dimension of reality in which each and every thing is identified and defined by relative positions and qualities.

The absolute: the dimension in which each and every thing is part of a seamless whole.

I often point to this by saying when we're thinking and acting as if we're a wave—particular, unique even, with a distinct direction, an observable beginning and end—all we see is a vast horizon of other waves that are basically crashing into one another all the time. That's living in the relative. When we're in touch with being the ocean, that's the absolute. In the absolute, all things share the same basic nature; are unified; are "empty" of inherent, independent, enduring self-essence. In the relative, there are important differences between things. Some are helpful; others are harmful. Everything that can be touched, sensed, conceived, or experienced is relative. In the absolute, nothing can be differentiated.

There are practical implications of our seeing things only from the relative point of view. We become aware, for instance, of the qualities and circumstances that define our individuality and affect our experience—the unique flavor of our lives and

99

personal karma. Still, it is also in a sense endlessly mundane, because everything in the relative is relatively ordinary, relatively unremarkable. In the absolute, there is no limitation by conditions, time, or space: It was before we were born and will be after we die. The absolute is sometimes referred to as the *suchness* or *thusness* of phenomena, which have absolute value given their unique place in the seamless whole, and are therefore "luminous and precious."

As we go on in this chapter to further explore some techniques to awaken practice in daily life, keep an eye out for how awareness is being shifted from absolute to relative, and where you may be habituated in one or the other. The facility to freely make that shift becomes more available the more we practice. With that facility, we encounter our life with greater clarity about who we really are and what's at play. Our frustrations and disappointments begin to teach and reveal. The great and obvious, as well as the small and the subtle, all begin to contribute to awakening.

Thresholds

Here's the full list of the Seven Thresholds that some of my students find helpful. They can be used simply as inner recitations to bring one to presence. (See Resources, page 122, if you'd like to order a frameable version.)

Some students also use them as koans, and we work together on how to realize and understand what each points to about the nature of self and reality. In this sense, they, like other koans, present "liminal" moments. (In anthropology, liminality is the ambiguity or disorientation that occurs in a rite of passage, when the pre-ritual state has been released, but the transition hasn't yet been made to the state available once the rite is complete. During a liminal stage, participants "stand at the threshold" between their previous way of structuring their identity, time, and community, and a newly awakened way.)

So, if you like, recognize these liminal moments by pausing and reciting one of the Seven Thresholds to yourself at the various thresholds of your day:

DAYSTART

This day of being blessed by blessing
being honored by honoring
being love by loving, I awaken

ORDINARY WATER

One taste, one life
this ordinary tap water
impossible to earn

INNER MEAL

The undivided life of all beings
I vow to taste, appreciate, and continue it
with wisdom and compassion

REAL WORK

Not knowing the full outcome of my effort
I will be generous, resilient, and creative in my service
And work to benefit life and relieve suffering

NO OTHER

The myriad ocean waves
each distinct and perfect
I meet myself in every being

SUNDOWN

Daylight ends;
darkness removes all difference
Exhaling, I am at ease

SLEEP

May this rest
reflect my trust in being
and faith in mind

Hairy Old Heart

When I was preparing to ordain as a Zen monastic, I understood the requirement to shave my head. I was a novice, several years into the discernment process, when Maezumi Roshi came to the monastery for a month. I respected him deeply and one day, after I'd presented several koans during the private meeting time (*dokusan;* heart-to-heart), he asked how I was doing relative to my upcoming ceremony.

I knew shaving the head was supposed to be about letting go of vanity and worldly agendas and putting the dharma and sangha in the center of one's life. I questioned the method, however, and shyly told him so. "I wouldn't poke out my eyes or pierce my eardrums to express commitment; why shave my hair off, which is like a sense organ to me? I know the wind when my hair lifts in a breeze; I swim and know the ocean as it moves through my hair." I went on and on then, saying it seemed more a male-centric confusion, thinking the body was somehow bad, making the physical out to be nothing but hindrance and provocation. . . .

When I finally wound down, he said quietly, "Not about hair, Myotai-san. Much more important: Shave the heart. Always shave the heart of ego, see?" Of course. That hairy old heart. . . . We left the meeting with the good kind of tears on both our faces.

And so consider this practice, irrespective of hairstyle: How do we shave the heart of ego? For men, perhaps as you shave each morning, link this question in as a practice. And for men or women, whenever we shampoo our hair, "the part we hold most high," can we also take a moment to notice how we may be "carrying the self forward," identifying, positively or negatively, with physical appearance? What would it be to let go a little, of whatever extra we're carrying, whether it veers in the direction of pride or dips into self-doubt? That shaved heart might notice the world a little bit more, don't you think?

The Gratitudinals

Imagine doing an exercise where one person is assigned to get up every morning and write down ten things they are unhappy about—basically to practice complaining. Another person is assigned, likewise, to get up every day and write a list, but in this case, to write down ten things they are grateful for, that support them and bring happiness or contentment. Imagine

WANTING IT

Bella is disabled with a very intense disease that increasingly limits her movement. When I first met her, she was in remission. We sat together a number of times, and then she had a very bad flare-up that had her bedbound and receiving home care services.

When I came to see her, she was very frustrated—like all of us who get stymied and can't do what we want to do, plus she was hurting. She explained, "I lie here and my mind just roils with thoughts and fears. Is it going to get worse? I try to be an 'adult,' but I'm so lonely and angry. I just don't want any of this!" After talking a bit, we did some breath practice, and she asked why I did this work of sitting with those who can't come to group sittings. I fessed up that I faced something a bit similar to her challenges, and I felt called to support others who otherwise would be alone in their practice.

I shared how I moved to a Zen monastery knowing that with my brand and degree of polyneuropathy, it was improbable that I could do the rigorous schedule. I'd been diagnosed when in my teens, and on good days my muscles usually felt like I had the flu. On bad days, I'd be out of commission with nerve pain. But there was a moment I just risked it: Since I'd likely have pain wherever I was, I might as well be where I could study. I was willing to be kicked out, but I wanted to give it my best shot. And it was hard, sometimes impossible, but also life-changing.

What happened at the monastery was that I learned how to practice. I learned how to trust myself (and others, too) to a degree I had lost track of being possible. I found my breath and, most importantly, zazen gave me a home in my heart-mind that transcended conditions or feelings. I wanted that for everyone who wanted it. Bella said, "I want it!" and smiled big. "We're on," I said, and rang the little bell to call us back to breath practice.

meeting these two people at the end of a year. You'd have, predictably, two very different people, two very different orientations and attitudes.

It's in this spirit that Zen centers usually chant the names of teachers throughout history. It's also why meals are made such a big deal of: Gratitude and vows to the future are celebrated on the occasion of receiving food.

One way to bring this practice home is to actually write down five to ten "fresh gratitudes" each morning. I say "fresh" to encourage coming up with items from that very day, the period since the last list was made. Recount a kindness, something beautiful, how you were supported, a taste. Just make a note, a few words that will trigger you to remember. People who like to write as part of their practice may want to spend ten to fifteen minutes writing out the list more fully, but the important thing is to just engage with your "gratitudinals." See where you are at the end of a year.

Fading Smoke

We live in the midst of dying. It has, of course, always been so. Yet in this generation, we're also witnessing the deaths of an alarming number of entire species in what many call the Sixth Great Extinction. Our grandchildren may never see a starfish, or thrill at a murmuration. To let this in is hard. Forests burn, storms worsen, people and animals are suffering. Many of us feel responsible, yet often mutely helpless.

One piece that often goes missing in our modern lives is the necessity to grieve. We can't show up to take care of what needs us, can't create the words and action the future asks of us, if our throats are choked with unspent tears and our bodies heavy with guilt, weighted down by loss.

Zen, as well as other long-standing religions, can support us in a practice of wakeful grieving together. If practicing in a more solitary way, we also become more honest when we make time to acknowledge loss.

One way to practice this is to light a stick of incense (just fill a small bowl with sand or rice, and place the lit stick in it), and bear witness for five to fifteen minutes as it burns away. Hold the being or beings that have died in mind, acknowledging their uniqueness, the gift of their life. As the wisp of smoke from the incense is palpable and fades, so it is with every life. This is not an easy practice and can feel awkward at first. Go through the awkwardness if you can. Trust that you can do this.

For perhaps several days or weeks, practice coming into simple, raw awareness of impermanence in this way, seeing and letting the smoke fade, and committing not to turn your gaze from how vulnerable—and precious—each life is.

Coffee Cup Practice

There's a beautiful moment in a Zen tea ceremony when the various implements that were just used to make and serve steaming cups of frothy green tea are brought out for the guests to see and appreciate. You get to really register the subtle indentations in the clay cup left by the hands that shaped it, sometimes a century or more ago. The makers' touch, the shape and warmth of her palms, are in your hands.

There are many opportunities to take up the ordinary objects that enable our days and to experience them fully. It only takes

RETIRING FROM THE EGO PROJECT

"Karen" was a regular at retreats and very devoted. I was surprised to see her in tears. She was very upset with another of the teachers and asked to see me. Earlier in the week, she'd met with her teacher, but she hadn't "passed the koan" she had been sitting with and over the days a drama had blossomed in her mind.

· "I'll never finish koan study at this rate; I'll never be empowered to open my own place and share the dharma, and that's all I want to do! There are complete assholes who have been given authority to teach, but I'm being held back! It's wrong!" As refreshing as I found this characterization of us teachers, she was distraught, angry, convinced not only that she was right, but owed something.

I listened, let her know I was deeply sorry she was suffering, and sent her back to talk with her teacher so there wouldn't be triangulation and confusion. Over the next several years of her practice, I'd see her settle in, and then become angry again whenever she "failed" or didn't get some sign of approval from the teacher. It was obvious she could someday serve as a generous provider of Zen study for others, but she might also spend her years angry, lost in a pretty classic case of what the Tibetan teacher Trungpa Rinpoche called "spiritual materialism."

The main point of any spiritual practice is to stop working for what we might call the Ego Project. Ego's need for comfort will "keep us in our crazy"—forever seeking the carrot of more spiritual, higher renditions of our self, as well as external validation. But to retire from the company, we only have to stop engaging with its promises. We're not going to get better, be other, arrive at a glorious goal. It's only when we stop turning practice into a method to "solve" our life, or get some "badge" testifying to our enlightenment, and make the radical gesture of sitting down squarely with our own pain, that our practice becomes our own. Ego is shrewd and resourceful—it can even masquerade as compassion and the desire to serve!

Eventually, this student did indeed sit down genuinely. Her practice helped her not be so afraid, and she cultivated wisdom and compassion for many, many years. The path and practice became her life, and attaining the goals she'd set for herself fell away. The Ego Project wasn't filling her with ambition.

She also, by the way, is now one of the "complete assholes" . . . a wonderful teacher leading her own community.

a minute or so, and it can be done without making a big deal of it. If you're a coffee drinker, try it with your favorite mug, or even the humble paper cup from the cafe that your morning brew came in. Without bringing judgment to it, just feel it. See the tint on the rim left by your lips, turn it so all angles are appreciated, without letting your mind dart away. And if you do find your mind wandering, acknowledge the thoughts, and for a few moments, keep bringing your attention back to the cup. It helps, by the way, not to be on your laptop: Just take a moment to "do nothing," to see and feel.

As "coffee cup practice" is repeated, over time it begins to open our senses to all sorts of little things we'd otherwise skim over in all our important rushing about. A cup of coffee becomes transformed into an opportunity to relax—a mini-meditation, a letting go of tension—rather than just a chemical jazzing up of our nervous system.

Love and Work

The two areas where most of us ordinary folk find the majority of our challenges are our work life and our love life. We tend to give them the most of our time and attention, and they deliver a major portion of the pain we experience. Though Zen is not a relationship improvement program or work skills training, it does provide some insight into what's at play. There are ways to engage love and work that are relatively cloudy and others that are relatively clear. How can we tilt toward the clearer end of the continuum?

When we see the world through the lens of our thoughts, everything is a little cloudy. We turn the people in our lives into ideas, what we think about them, rather than actually being with them. Unintentionally, we can kind of degrade our colleagues by engaging them in terms of what we presume we know about them, because we stop being actually present. The good thing is that this can be turned around. Below are a few very brief exercises that demonstrate how practice can help loosen the grip thought has on how we're relating. Use them as little bridges when you recognize you've become stuck.

NOT DEFINED BY

Most conflict has at its core a frustration of love. We know in our bones that we need one another, that this human life comes down to love, and yet here is someone intent on hurting us, or oblivious to our needs, or doing harm to someone else. Love and affection are the last emotions we're likely to have at such a moment. Yet the pain in our being arises because we know love is possible, and it has been disappointed or betrayed.

To work on this first requires, again, directly acknowledging the pain. All good art and all honest practice starts here. Don't retell the story: You already know it. I'll repeat that for emphasis: Stop telling yourself the story of what's going on. Just breathe; be the pain for a moment. Shift your breath to elongate the exhale. Take five elongated breaths in this way.

Now allow the thought: *I am not defined by my pain or this situation.*

Just that, for five to ten breaths.

WORK, NOT JOB

Work is a field where fear hides in the bushes. It's where failure bites at our ankles, along with loss and disgrace. Impermanence taints even the greatest of accomplishments, which then whisper things about death that we'd really like not to hear.

One very quick practice: Center, breathe, then exhale and allow the thought *My real work is not defined by my job.* Obviously, nothing happens just by repeating words to yourself. It is only when we begin to break the habit of living in the story, or as if this is all a fill-in-the-blank test with right answers, that things shift. The mind will want to fill in that blank, give you an immediate answer to *So, what is my "real work" then?* But whatever answer you give creates an idea, and what we're talking about is not that. The key is to just hold the question, open and real and raw.

Epilogue

*Pour nous tous . . . revenons à nos moutons!**

*This expression is used when conversation has strayed from the original topic, and literally means *Let's get back to our sheep*! It actually means *Let's get back to the point*! It derives from French literature, from a tale called "la Farce du Maître Pathelin," written by Rabelais in the fifteenth century. The protagonist of this medieval play brings two cases before a judge, one about sheep and the other about sheets. While arguing the sheep case, Maître Pathelin regularly brings up sheets in order to confuse the judge, who tries to get back to the first case each time by saying *"Mais revenons à nos moutons!"* And so, *moutons* came to symbolize the subject at hand.

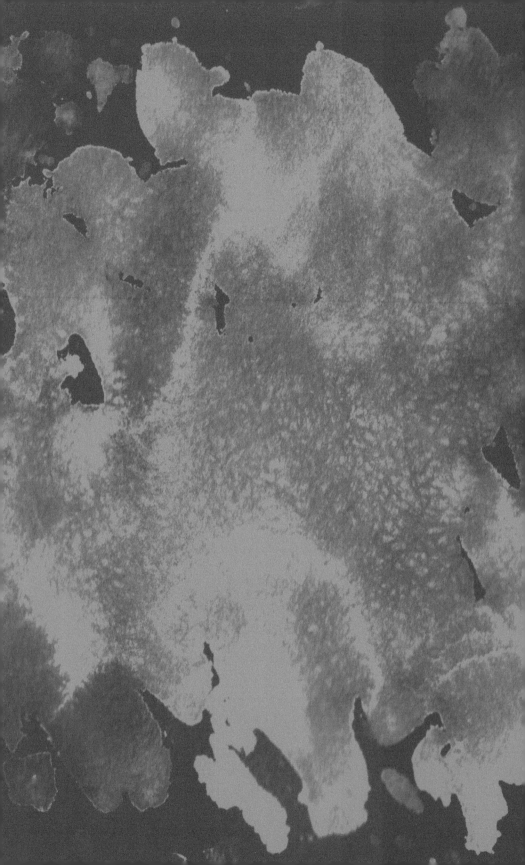

Trusting Mind

Below is a Dharma Talk on a Zen koan given by Myotai Sensei.
Dharma Talks are usually presented in a zendo (meditation hall)
after several periods of meditation. An announcement would be made
that certain aspects of Dharma Talks may be "dark to the mind, but
radiant to the heart," encouraging everyone to hear the presentation
not just intellectually, but also with the possibility of waking up to the
wisdom and compassion at the heart of all things.

A seemingly very simple koan from the Mumonkan collection:
Yunmen asked his community: "The world is vast and wide.
Why put on your robe at the sound of a bell?" That's the whole
koan, nothing more nor less than that statement and question.
Like all the best koans, it doesn't argue or explain much, but
expresses instead what we might call an uncanny trust.

The koan trusts our capacity to realize vibrantly and uniquely
the truth of our essential freedom. Unfortunately, because trust
is such a rare experience nowadays, many of us don't know how
to receive it. We get squirmy, or vaguely angry that we're not
being given the answer. Something's not right here, we'll quietly
insist; something's missing. We hunger for "the teaching," as if
it were dead meat, not the living beast. But Yunmen is regarded

as a kind of spiritual genius in the history of Zen, largely because of his "live words"—the way he teaches without giving us anything. Why doesn't he give? Because we're not lacking. He trusts that this is so because he's experienced it, and knows the same experience is directly available to us.

The world changes when we begin to appreciate that Yunmen—and countless teachers since—have bothered to bring up this matter at all. They bother to poke healthy flesh, to shake the sleeping. There's a generosity at work in this koan that has awakened students for centuries. We keep that generosity flowing when we practice, which is simply that trust manifesting. So, let's look at what Yunmen is up to.

The temple bell cuts through the silence of morning zazen. Dawn is breaking. The birds are calling. With the ringing of the large metal bell, chanting begins around you—in you. As you place your folded robe on your head, the soft weight presses against your skin. Invoking your vows, you unfold the cloth and wrap it around you, covering your left shoulder. The chanting fades. Why, the koan asks, given the endless possibilities for a new day, given this "fresh dawn," put on this robe?

The robe in question here is a monastic robe, because Yunmen was working with monastics, and this is what they did every morning. In this koan, he used the particulars of his own time and place. But regardless of when and where we live, each of us—lay practitioner and monastic—puts on the clothes of the day. We wear what we wear; we do what we do. So, although in one sense Yunmen is challenging his students about their monastic vows, the challenge is more basic. We're asked, if we're to take up this koan honestly, to first see whether, indeed, the "world is vast and wide." The world and the self—is there a line between them that would make each partial, limited, fundamentally dualistic? If so, then "vast" is a bit of an overstatement, don't you think? But if that line can't be drawn—and Buddhists for centuries have noticed that when they look for that line they can't find it—what are the implications?

This is the first entry point into the koan: realizing the unbounded. Placing ourselves in reality, where we've always been, however unaware. This is where zazen itself opens the door, revealing what we've perhaps spent a lifetime trying to hide. To take up a koan outside of zazen can be a little like trying to explain the color blue to someone who's always been blind. Blue is there, but no way to see it has been developed. One glimpse, and suddenly all those songs about blue skies can stir in you in ways you couldn't imagine before.

Zazen is critical.

I haven't met anyone in long-term Zen training who hasn't gone through times when they step away from zazen, only to find that their "life song," if you will, has become abstract, distant from the vitality they once accessed when sitting meditation was a part of every day. Even the great, charismatic voices of the spirit, if they're not drawing directly from the unbounded, begin to move us less deeply. It's as if they're teaching something they remember, not something as immediate as a taste on the tongue. I can't encourage us too strongly to make zazen a daily practice. Even though no one has ever sufficiently explained why it makes a difference, it does. Maybe it's enough to just say that beyond mental focus and the discipline of letting passing thoughts actually pass and not become obsessions—inarguably helpful capacities to develop—there is a direct expression in zazen of the unbounded mind. Without zazen, it's just too easy to tacitly wait for our real life to begin. "It's alive!" as they always used to say in those great sci-fi movies in the 1950s, poking some lump with a probe and leaping back. The next scene, Yunmen whispers, is up to you.

Okay, so the daybreak of each moment is vast and boundless, Yunmen says. Now what? We're left alone with this one, and no teacher can give us anything but their trust in our capacity, alone in a world that is boundless. "I, alone between heaven and earth," the Buddha said, enlightened by—and enlightening—the morning star. Transforming the habitual loneliness of separation into the true aloneness of intimacy is the fundamental human project, our real life's work. That transformation frees us to love without depending on response or gratitude. It frees us to do what we're called to do without hedging the bet, limiting the risk.

A student of mine had been told he was likely to die. His pancreas was basically melting, and his body was raging with fever and breaking down in what seemed like endless ways, with every day bringing something new and horrible. Then he hit a period of remission. He found himself aware that he was ready to die, having developed a certain peace with that knowledge. Then someone asked him if he was equally ready to live—and whether his son might not need him to stay alive if he could.

He wrote, "All through my practice I thought what was driving me was my fear of death. At that moment, I realized what I was actually afraid of was really living."

I'm happy to report that he then essentially began to "kick butt," as they say, and reorganized his treatment team. He has come back not only to full functioning, but to a frankly frightening vigor. And you can't get away with the slightest insincerity with him.

Real koans, whether we find them in our body or in an old collection from Zen's history, are like that, so bare to the bone,

so unclouded by excess, that to meet their demand we have
to be almost unbearably spare. We can't carry anything into
the room, any protection, any buffer. As with death, we stand
suddenly naked and alone. After a shared tragedy, people are
washed clear for a while, after the wringing grip of intense
grief. We are left with this sparseness—a tenderness that is
practically edgeless. When the mental clutter begins to reas-
semble, many find themselves grieving not only for the dead,
but also for the passing of that quality of spare tenderness.
Daily routines can heal, but they can also put our hearts to
sleep. Grief will continue to change us, to take another turn.
Wisdom will call us to express really living in increasingly vital,
compassionate, and creative ways. Distraction and confusion
will call us to despair and depression. Sitting clearly in our lives,
we'll notice the possibilities of each call. We'll be able to manifest according to trust, rather than fear. Just be awake, and
strength and clarity will find you. Don't try to get through by
losing yourself in rote activity, or by ignoring what you feel. Be
awake, returning again and again to the moment.

Yunmen's koan is haunting: when we press the what, the
why, and the how, we live our lives in the context of vastness.
One of the classic descriptions of the training period we call
Ango is "pure, vast, genuine, ocean gathering." The image is
helpful to an extent. We can imagine an all-water universe,
in which individual beings are the waves, and the vastness of
being is the ocean. We can take a wave's-eye view, and know
how a wave may "think" whatever it does doesn't matter. It's
"going" nowhere, because it's an all-water world. It may "feel"
peaceful about its situation or "believe" that it's all pointless and
sad. Then imagine the ocean's-eye view, along with the wave's
continuity within it, and the wave "realizing" it is none other

than the mighty ocean itself. Can we imagine the boundless life of that wave—endlessly, intimately realizing every trough and rise of the sea? What is that? Without resorting to the image of the water-world—or an explanation of any variety—can we respond vitally to Yunmen's koan, to the koan of our life? What is it to not be a robot, to not go on automatic, to not be lost in an ocean of pointlessness? "It's all very well," Aitken Roshi once wrote, "to contain the vast, wide world. It's all very well to cast off body and mind and find Mu everywhere. But can you step from a 100-foot pole without falling on your face?"

Mumon, the teacher who collected these koans of the ancient masters, added a commentary which reminds us not to reside in an understanding that's too superficial, but to cull the koan's subtleties: "All you Zen students training in the Way, don't be victimized by sounds; don't be blinded by forms," he said. "You may have realization on hearing a sound or awaken on seeing a form; this is natural. But don't you know that real living Zen students can ride sounds and veil forms? They will see all and sundry clearly. They handle each and every thing deftly. Perhaps you are such a person, but tell me: does the sound come to the ear, or does the ear go to the sound? And if you have transcended sound and silence, what do you say at such a point? If you listen with your ear, it's hard to understand. If you hear with your eye, you are intimate at last." Dogen Zenji works the same edge in his Genjokoan: "That the self advances and confirms the ten thousand things is called delusion. That the ten thousand things advance and confirm the self is enlightenment."

There are echoes of this in Colin Wilson's book *Poetry and Mysticism*, published some fifty years ago and just full of attitude, or what an old professor of mine once called "the necessary piss and vinegar." Wilson critiques what he calls the "passive fallacy" in literature and life: "Most wild creatures are under the protection of their parents for a very brief period, then they are out in the world. By comparison, human beings spend a very long period being fed, clothed and educated. That is, being more or less passive. The period in which a small bird opens its beak and has worms dropped into it lasts only a month or so. The period in which human beings open their mouths and expect food may last 20 years or so. This encourages a habit of passivity, and the habit becomes very deeply engrained. Moments of sudden intense happiness are accepted as a gift from nature. And this habit of passivity leads to the total loss of motivation." Wilson rails against writers who were "children of opulence," like Proust, who was spoiled, as he freely admits in his novel, and who consequently "spent his life like a bird with its mouth open; coming to believe that life was hostile because it refused to supply him with worms."

As a student of poetry and the tradition of literary criticism, I loved Wilson, but it took years to let what he was teaching really have its deeper impact. Could it be that the world is not hostile just because we're not getting what we think we need to be happy? Could that be so, even in the world we live in now, with its atrocities and disappointments? What is the world? And what happens when we stop waiting for the worm to be delivered?

This is the koan Yunmen gave his monks, to make sure they didn't settle into some dharma nest. It is the koan entrusted to us as well, in every moment. We have everything we need to realize it. Dig into boundless mind with zazen, and don't wait to feel some other way in order to sit down in the center of your life. That sparseness in your plain heart: just put your trust right there, and live.

Resources

OTHER BOOKS BY BONNIE MYOTAI TREACE

Winter Moon: A Season of Zen
A collection of dharma talks by Zen teacher Bonnie Myotai
Treace, Sensei, touching on topics from koans to poetry,
ancient Buddhist masters to contemporary issues.

Empty Branches: A Season of Zen
Explores how the ancient stories of Zen (koans) can support
more genuine encounters with one another, oneself, the
earth, and all creatures.

*To order a Hermitage Heart Just-the-Right-Amount bowl
or frameable copy of the Seven Thresholds, contact:
https://www.hermitageheartzenbmt.com*

BOOKS

Zen Mind, Beginner's Mind
Shunryu Suzuki
In the thirty years since its original publication, *Zen Mind,
Beginner's Mind* has become one of the great modern Zen
classics. It's a book to come back to time and time again as
an inspiration to practice.

**Zen Women: Beyond Tea Ladies, Iron Maidens, and
Macho Masters**
Grace Schireson
This landmark presentation at last makes heard the centuries
of Zen's female voices. Through exploring the teachings and

history of Zen's female ancestors, a more balanced dharma practice is presented.

Mindful Eating: A Guide to Rediscovering a Healthy and Joyful Relationship with Food
Dr. Jan Bays
Drawing on recent research and integrating her experiences as a physician and meditation teacher, Dr. Jan Bays offers a wonderfully clear presentation of what mindfulness is and how it can help with food issues.

The World Could Be Otherwise: Imagination and the Bodhisattva Path
Norman Fischer
In an inspiring reframe of classic Buddhist teachings, Zen teacher Norman Fischer writes that the paramitas, or "six perfections"—generosity, ethical conduct, patience, joyful effort, meditation, and understanding—can help us reconfigure the world we live in.

Waking Up to What You Do: A Zen Practice for Meeting Every Situation with Intelligence and Compassion
Diane Eshin Rizzetto
Using the Zen Precepts as tools to develop a keen awareness of the motivations behind every aspect of our behavior—to "wake up to what we do"—from moment to moment.

The Eight Gates of Zen: A Program of Zen Training
John Daido Loori
This accessible introduction to the philosophy and practice of Zen Buddhism includes a program of study that encompasses practically every aspect of life.

MEDITATION APPS

Headspace
headspace.com
Designed to make meditation accessible to secular audiences, particularly those who have never meditated before. Useful timer for scheduling meditation and receiving reminder notification at set times. Some may find it overly simplified.

The Mindfulness App
themindfulnessapp.com
Timed Sessions: guided and silent meditations, from 3 to 30 minutes; customizable meditation with guided introduction, bells, and nature sounds; meditation reminders to help stay mindful throughout the day.

Calm
calm.com
Calming exercises, breathing techniques to help you relax, walking meditation, and a Calm Kids section with meditations for kids between 3 and 17. Works with Apple Watch.

Buddhify
buddhify.com
More than 200 meditations to reduce anxiety and stress, promote sleep, and manage difficult emotions.

10% Happier
tenpercent.com
Designed for "skeptics"; new content added weekly. Daily videos and guided meditations.

Insight Timer
insighttimer.com
Thousands of guided meditations, discussion groups, music tracks, and ambient sounds to calm the mind and promote sleep.

ONLINE TEACHING/TRAINING

wwzc.org/long-distance-training-program
White Wind Zen Community's Long-distance Training Program was established in 1995 at Dainen-ji, the monastery founded by Ven. Anzan Hoshin.

www.vineobstacleszen.com/moodle/
Vine of Obstacles offers Zen practice under the guidance of a senior Zen teacher, Dōshō Port.

https://zenstudiespodcast.com
The Zen Studies podcast with Domyo Burk, a Soto Zen priest.

https://zmm.org/media
Zen Mountain Monastery podcasts and other resources.

GROUP PRACTICE CENTERS

Zen Centers in the US
iriz.hanazono.ac.jp/zen_centers/centers_data/
usaNW.htm
Sorted by state, city, and center name; compiled in 2000.

Soto Zen Buddhist Association

szba.org

Soto Zen is one of the two major Japanese Zen schools; this list provides contacts for their major centers in the United States.

Mountains and Rivers Order

zmm.org

Western Zen Buddhist lineage established by the late John Daido Loori, Roshi. Monastery and Temple in New York, with affiliate groups worldwide.

The Kwan Um School of Zen

kwanumzen.org

International community of Zen centers, close to 100 locations, founded by Korean teacher Seung Sahn.

Buddhanet

buddhanet.net

Lists various Zen Buddhist websites, blogs, and centers.

Index

Women, 37–38, 68–69, 85
Work, 81, 85–87, 110–112
Wu-men, 4

Z

Zafu (sitting cushion), 57
Zazen
  about, 8, 55–60
  beginning instruction in,
    38, 41–42, 56–58
  being present, 61–62
  breathing, 60–61
  developing a practice, 62–63
  posture, 58–60
  sitting, 74–76
Zen
  about, 1–2, 6–7, 9
  misconceptions about, 2–4
  practice, 34–38
  way, 99–100

Acknowledgments

Really, it's all my fault.

It is said that if someone attempts to explain Zen, their eyebrows will fall out. There's also a revered tradition in Zen of offering apologies after a presentation. So, to those whose life and teachings inspired me, profound apology for the inadequacy of all herein. Your willingness to err in kind inspired me down to my bones. Thank you for your eyebrows.

Specifically: John Daido Loori, whose Beginning Instruction lecture was the most important half hour of my life. And for finding that mountain, and loving it and all who came there so well. And Shishin Wick, my Preceptor, whose heart seems always so still and clear. My thanks to Peter Matthiessen for insisting that we go through the entire koan curriculum, again, during dokusan out in his garden with the wind ruffling our robes. For Pema Chodron, who lingered over tea, wrote the best letters in the history of time, and could roar while whispering. I trust you as much as the Cape Breton shore rocks. And the great Rabbi Zalman Schachter-Shalomi, famed founder of the Jewish Renewal movement, for giving me the name Hannah and winking as he said now I was "the protector of prayer" . . . and for that hour-long healing tape you took the time to make and send to me when I was wiped out with post–Lyme disease pain. You were compassion in spades. And Rabbi David Ingber, for those early conversations about everything and nothing, about how to best serve, and of course, the chicken.

I'd like to also acknowledge and thank the gorgeous spirit and presence of women teachers of Buddhism. To say "they persist" is to understate the challenges. I thank Tsultrim Allione, for her brilliance and commitment, and also for modeling the dignity of presenting the dharma just by the way she crosses a room. When you walked into the dining hall at the monastery, it was the first time I saw a woman occupy space with no remnant of apology or ego, and it changed the way I stood on earth. My gratitude for Chozen Bays, for showing up with tremendous kindness always, particularly when the conversations were running in the other direction, and being willing to enter the fray. And to Grace Schireson, for your friendship ("You're not wearing that hat are you, Myotai?"), scholarship, and astonishing integrity. Thank you for all you've done to shine a light on the feisty females of the Way. My gratitude to Joan Halifax, for your coyote-howl, the permeability of your presence, and all that your deep intelligence has brought to the dharma. Special thanks as well to dharma sister Enkyo O'Hara, for walking alongside, for charging ahead, for hanging back. You are a true cowgirl and someone who sees, gives wholeheartedly, and never forgets that there's a joke of sorts at the center of it all. I also am grateful to Gesshin Greenwood, who arrived on the teaching scene with a synthesizing wit that is like fresh air. And back around 1850, the Zen nun Rengetsu wrote and made pottery and fed the poor. Finding your work, Ren, when I was in my hut in the woods during my exile of a sort, set my mind on fire even as it chilled all anxiety. Thank you for going rogue, making art and making art and making art, no matter what. You saved me.

Special thanks as well for the sincerity and perseverance of all those who've studied with me. Your lives are the great teachings, and your willingness to engage inspires me nonstop.

I'd also like to apologize to my beloved, Rob, for every time I didn't meet you well. Your talent for encouragement, and the daily-ness of creating home and practice, leave me speechless.

So, though there are a zillion more apologies owed and gratitudes to express, I should shut up now. But a few remaining notes have to be sounded: Resa Alboher and Alice Peck for your penetrating insights about writing, editors Vanessa Ta and Ruby Privateer at Rockridge Press for your good ideas and attention to detail, and finally, my mom, who gave me sets of bookends for birthday presents every year for years and years "to hold all the books (I) should get busy writing." Okay, Mom.

About the Author

Bonnie Myotai Treace is a Zen priest, poet of meager renown, and ardent feminist. For many years she was a Zen teacher, or sensei, at Zen Mountain Monastery (as Vice Abbot) and the Zen Center of New York City (as Abbot). She is presently founder and spiritual director of Hermitage Heart Zen. No longer a bald monk but a gray-haired crone (*irritant*), she is particularly fond of 7 a.m., when the fog softens up the edges of the Blue Ridge Mountains. Many of her students are artists, writers, and other loner types, including those who, due to illness or disability, find retreat attendance difficult. She has written two previous books, *Winter Moon* and *Empty Branches*, and her teachings have appeared in various collected works and Buddhist publications and have been featured several times in *The Best Buddhist Writing*. She lives with her husband (along with the famous cat, Mr. Chickabee, and his servant, Abby, the gigantic collie) near Black Mountain, North Carolina.

CPSIA information can be obtained
at www.ICGtesting.com
Printed in the USA
BVHW020925031019
560124BV00009B/28/P